FAKE QUERY LETTERS BY DEAD AUTHORS

by David Griffin Brown
and Michelle Barker

PRAISE FOR IMMERSION & EMOTION

"Michelle Barker and David Griffin Brown have crafted a literary gem that deserves a permanent spot on every writer's bookshelf."

"This book is a treasure trove for both aspiring writers and seasoned authors, offering profound insights into the art of creating immersive and emotionally resonant narratives."

⭐ ⭐ ⭐ ⭐ ⭐

"If you aspire to craft stories that captivate and resonate, this book is an indispensable companion."

⭐ ⭐ ⭐ ⭐ ⭐

"'Immersion and Emotion' has been truly transformative for my writing journey."

⭐ ⭐ ⭐ ⭐ ⭐

"Clear, concise, and jam-packed with practical insight for writers."

⭐ ⭐ ⭐ ⭐ ⭐

"This book is one that will remain close at hand for reference."

⭐ ⭐ ⭐ ⭐ ⭐

"I highly recommend it for writers of all skill levels."

⭐ ⭐ ⭐ ⭐ ⭐

"Michelle and David have compiled the definitive book on how to write a powerful novel."

Darling Axe Publishing

DarlingAxe.com

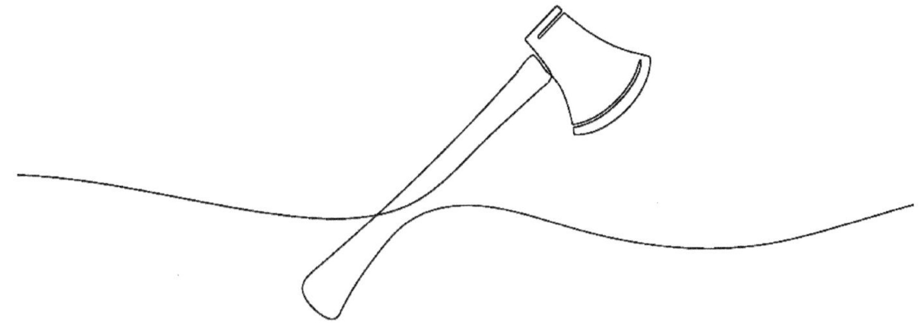

Copyright © 2026 Michelle Barker

Copyright © 2026 David Griffin Brown

ISBN: 978-1-7380766-8-0

Cover designed by MiblArt.com.

Contents

Introduction 1

Part One: Fake Query Letters 5

Part Two: Fake Synopses 29

Part Three: (Not Fake) First Pages 53

Part Four: Query Quest 71

In Conclusion: Keep Writing 130

Appendix 1: Resource Reviews 133

Appendix 2: Let's Get Personal............................ 137

About the Authors.. 141

Introduction

First Things First: Who the Heck Are We?

Hello, fellow storytellers! We are David Brown and Michelle Barker, senior editors at the Darling Axe. We met in the MFA program at the University of British Columbia, then joined forces in 2018. Since then, we've written two craft books, coached a ton of clients, reviewed thousands of contest entries, presented at a whack of conferences, and interviewed over 100 literary agents.

On top of all this, we're both authors. That means we know what it's like to tear our hair out—aka send our work out into the world, only to be rejected over, and over, and over again. You really do have to love the craft to endure the kind of punishment that awaits all writers.

The key is finding joy in the process. And since querying agents is part of that process, our premise is that there is joy to be found there too... somewhere.

How to Use This Book

FAKE QUERY LETTERS BY DEAD AUTHORS is intended to transform your querying strategies by using a hands-on approach to familiar works so that you can see the process in action. Think of it as a college-level course rather than a quick resource—and hopefully more fun than college.

The book is chiefly for novelists seeking an agent or publisher. However, since memoirs are pitched in pretty much the same way as novels, the process will work for you memoirists as well. Nonfiction book proposals are a completely different beast. Entire books have been written on how to approach those. This is not one of them.

We will start by stepping into an agent's shoes to review some query letters and synopses that we've devised based on classic novels, along with their (not fake) opening pages. Then we'll discuss the (sometimes harsh) realities of querying today. Along the way, we include activities to help you consider your manuscript from a stranger's perspective—or even from the perspective of the market. If you want an agent to represent you, the first step is to ensure that your manuscript serves the reader's experience. The reader comes first—because, naturally, you want to sell books.

(Side note: even if you're querying small presses rather than agents, these principles apply.)

Why Dead Authors?

Reason number one: it's no accident that classics have endured, so we've created a series of fake (and intentionally awful) query letters and synopses by literary ghosts to use as examples of how an author can go wrong with their presentation and pitch. We'll then revise them to give them a fighting chance in today's market.

Reason number two: these classics are all in the public domain. So... fair game!

We will be looking at:

- *Pride and Prejudice*, by Jane Austen
- *Wuthering Heights*, by Emily Brontë
- *The Scarlet Letter*, by Nathaniel Hawthorne
- *Anne of Green Gables*, by Lucy Maud Montgomery
- *Jane Eyre*, by Charlotte Brontë

If you haven't read these novels, fear not. Even if you did plow through them in university and hoped never to revisit them again, you don't have to be nervous. We'll be approaching them as if we are agents working through a slush pile. Meaning, we're pretending we haven't read them either; we're just getting the pitch. Each of them offers valuable insights into what makes a pitch stand out and how even a classic, if on query today, might make an agent cry for all the wrong reasons.

Of course, it's important to acknowledge that this is an exercise and that these novels were all written for very different audiences. Readers today have different expectations and concerns, so to a certain extent we must consider these works as historical fiction. Yes, this is all hypothetical, but we're still asking those critical questions about resonance and relevance: Does it work? Do we care?

That said, these novels have stood the test of time. Circumstances and politics might change, but human nature remains the same over the centuries (which is why we still love *Romeo and Juliet*). Since we want our own work to endure beyond flavour of the month, it's worth looking at books that have managed to accomplish that.

A Preliminary Note from the Trenches

Submitting your work can be such a soul-deadening experience that after five rejections it's tempting to throw up your hands and say, "See? I knew my novel was crap."

According to agent Noah Lukeman, the throwing-up-hands stage shouldn't start until you're at submission number fifty at least.

Here are some statistics to consider:

- It took Agatha Christie five years to find someone who would publish her novels.
- The *Chicken Soup for the Soul* series (okay, not a personal favourite, but bear with us) went to 140 publishers before it found a home.
- "Nobody will want to read a book about a seagull," one editor told Richard Bach. *Jonathan Livingston Seagull* ended up selling forty-four million copies.
- *A Wrinkle in Time* was rejected twenty-six times, *The Time Traveler's Wife* twenty-five times, and *The Help* sixty times.

When Stephen King was starting out as a writer, he pounded a nail into his wall on which he kept all his rejection letters. Soon the nail was too small to hold them, so he replaced it with a spike—and kept on writing and kept on sending out his work.

The rest, as they say, is history.

Hearing the word no isn't fun, but it's a necessary part of the process. As Ernest Hemingway said, "The first draft of anything is shit." The second or third draft might still be a little smelly.

The point here (and we'll keep coming back to it) is that in order to succeed, you cannot give up. But that doesn't mean relentlessly sending the same query letter and sample pages to every agent on QueryTracker. Not giving up means continual reassessment and revision—honing your query so it starts attracting positive responses and, eventually, that coveted book deal or representation.

So, let's get started.

A Secondary Note About These Queries

You're about to read some pretty terrible query letters and synopses, and you might be thinking, *I would never do those things*. Maybe not. But you might be shocked to hear what aspiring authors have tried to catch an agent's attention—from flower deliveries to singing telegrams.

Everything you're about to read in the query letters that follow has been done in some form by an author looking for representation. Prepare yourself.

What Makes a Good Query Letter?

The query letter is essentially the sales pitch for your novel. It's your chance to demonstrate to an editor or agent that you have a good idea *and* you've executed it skillfully (in theory at least, since the real proof comes in the writing). It shows that you know where your book might sit on a bookstore shelf. You know why the world needs this novel and why you're the person to write it.

This is your knock on the door, your moment to explain the most pertinent information about your story and convince someone to invest time in reading it, so you don't want to squander your big chance. First impressions, after all, are key, and agents and publishers are busy people. They see A LOT of crappy query letters. You need to make sure yours isn't one of them.

With that in mind, it's time to enter the Fake Deads universe. We have channelled the spirits of several literary giants and imagined what their query letters might have looked like if they were sending out their work today. We'll start with a dud, then look at the revision. As we proceed, put on your hypothetical agent hat. Think about what's working in these letters, what isn't, what you might emulate, and what you might improve upon.

Fake Query #1: Pride and Prejudice

Overview

Jane Austen's *Pride and Prejudice* (1813) has given us a heartthrob legacy in Elizabeth Bennet, Mr. Darcy, and about two hundred years of romantic misunderstandings in adaptations ranging from stage plays to zombies. But in the Fake Deads alternate universe you've just entered, Jane Austen is just another aspiring novelist cold-emailing agents, certain her debut will set the world on fire—if only she can figure out how to write a query letter.

Spoiler alert: she can't.

Jane Austen's (Fake) Query Letter

Dear Agent,

I hope this is okay to send—I know you must be very busy. I've been trying to finish my novel, *Pride and Prejudice*, but I thought I'd better query now before you fill up your list. It's around 110,000 words so far, though the ending is still coming together.

It's about pride, prejudice, first impressions, misunderstandings, marriage, and how society can be very unfair sometimes. I promise it all makes sense in the book.

Readers who enjoyed *Pamela* or *Belinda* will probably like it, though maybe my book isn't as good as those.

I did write another book called *Sense and Sensibility*. Some people liked it.

Anyway, thank you so much for reading this. I hope it isn't a waste of your time.

Yours truly,

Jane Austen

Bad Query Bingo Card

Jane Austen's query letter hits a number of squares on the Bad Query Bingo Card for several reasons. Here's the breakdown:

Insecure tone: Hedging has no place in what is essentially a business proposal. *I hope this isn't a waste of your time?* Agents want confidence, not an apology tour.

Incomplete manuscript: Querying before you finish will fast-track your manuscript to the trash folder. Agents get their pick from thousands of queries per year. Most of their time is devoted to their current clients. That means an ideal new client will have a manuscript that is as polished as possible. Finished? Goes without saying (but we're saying it anyway). But also, the book should be well out of the first-draft stage.

Too short: This letter ends before it even gets started. A query isn't the same as an elevator pitch. It should provide a professional introduction to the story's hook, stakes, and characters. One page is the standard length (around 350 words, if you're sending an email). A little shorter is fine. Longer than one page is not.

Outdated comps: Yes, *Pamela* and *Belinda* were Austen's real-life inspirations. But in our Fake Deads scenario, she's querying today. Agents use comps not for the sake of comparison but as a demonstration that you are actively reading within your market and therefore know your manuscript's place within it. That means choosing mid-list titles that have come out in the last two to three years.

Word count red flag: 110,000 words for a debut romance screams "needs editing." Most agents expect something closer to 75–90k for this genre. (In fact, *Pride and Prejudice* is closer to 120k words.)

Scant bio: Austen mentions *Sense and Sensibility* but doesn't sell it. If you have a previous publication, show what it accomplished—sales, reviews, awards. Anything besides "some people liked it." If, however, it tanked, it might be better not to mention it.

"Dear Agent": For the purposes of our Fake Deads analysis, we'll start all the query letters with *Dear Agent.* However, keep in mind that a query letter should be addressed to a specific person (whom you've chosen with care). That tiny bit of personalization is crucial—and make sure to spell their name correctly. In fact, some agents appreciate even more of a personal touch. We'll go into this topic more in Part Four: Query Quest.

Take Two: The Revision

Dear Agent,

I'm seeking representation for *Pride and Prejudice*, a historical romance complete at 92,000 words.

When the wealthy Mr. Bingley leases a neighbouring estate, Mrs. Bennet is determined that one of her five daughters will marry him—or someone like him. Sparks fly when Bingley falls for Jane Bennet, the eldest and kindest of the girls, while his proud friend Mr. Darcy clashes with Jane's witty sister, Elizabeth. What begins as a battle of pride and first impressions soon unravels into a story of scandal, second chances, and the search for love in a world where financial security often trumps happiness.

With its mix of romance, social satire, and high stakes for the Bennet family's future, *Pride and Prejudice* will appeal to readers of historical romance that blends heart and humour. Comparable titles include *A Lady's Guide to Scandal* by Sophie Irwin (2023) and *An Heiress's Guide to Deception and Desire* by Manda Collins (2021), both novels with witty heroines navigating romance amid the expectations of Regency society.

My previous novel, *Sense and Sensibility*, was praised for its humour and insight into family dynamics and continues to reach new readers today. Alongside my fiction, I've published short pieces in *The Lady's Magazine* and maintain a growing readership online for my serialized stories.

Thank you for your time and consideration. I would be delighted to send the full manuscript at your request.

Sincerely,

Jane Austen

If you were an agent and this landed on your desk...

Let's imagine this query hits your inbox on a Monday morning. Coffee in hand, you skim the pitch: five sisters, various suitors, and one mother determined to marry them all off. The pitch promises wit, romance, and social commentary layered with personal misunderstandings.

How does this concept strike you if you're reading as a modern agent, juggling dozens of submissions? How does it compare to the other historical romances that tend to land in your slush pile?

Overall, this is a strong pitch. The romantic engine is obvious—the Lizzy/Darcy tension practically sells itself—and the backdrop of family obligation and class expectations hints at some strong plot complications. Most readers love a romance that says something about the world as well as the heart, so the promise of banter mixed with a sharp eye on gender and class has appeal.

But we also have to weigh logistics. A word count over 90k is still high for this genre, and while the romantic setup is charming, the market is crowded with Regency romances. So agents will want a hint of what sets this one apart. Is it the prose style? The feminist bite? The scandal potential?

Even so, Austen gives us more than enough reason to turn to the writing sample for a closer look. That, after all, is the true test.

Fake Query #2: Wuthering Heights

Overview

Emily Brontë's *Wuthering Heights* (1847) drags us straight onto the wild, wind-battered Yorkshire moors, where love and revenge tangle across two generations of Earnshaws and Lintons. At its centre sits Heathcliff, an orphan with a volcanic temper, and Catherine Earnshaw, whose devotion to him burns as fiercely as it destroys. Their love story (or maybe their hate story?) unleashes a cycle of jealousy, obsession, and ghosts both real and metaphorical.

Brontë filters this chaos through two narrators: the hapless Mr. Lockwood, who mostly wishes he'd booked a different rental, and Nelly Dean, the housekeeper with a front-row seat to decades of family drama. The result is a gothic cocktail of passion, cruelty, and one very memorable haunted windowpane.

In the Fake Deads universe, though, Brontë isn't a literary icon. She's a debut author hoping this windswept tale of love and vengeance will stand out in an agent's inbox—if only her query letter doesn't get lost in the storm.

Emily Brontë's (Fake) Query Letter

Dear Agent,

I know you don't usually except this Genre, but I figured my book deserves an exception.

My novel, Wuthering Heights (working tittle), is a gothic romance novel with about 116,000 words, give or taken. It tells the story of Heathcliff and Catherine, two people who love each other to deaths but are torn apart by social standings, miss understandings, and the cruel brand of fate. Their love ignites a never-ending cycle of revenge that effects not just them but there children's children's children.

The story is narrated by Mr. Lockwood, a landlord who gets stuck between a rock and the wrong place, and Mrs. Nelly Dean, a housekeeper who has been the eye of the storm for generations. Through they're voices, we uncover passion, anger, hatred, and sometimes ghosts.

If you liked *Where the Crawdads Sing* or *The Night Circus*, you will find my book very much identical. Those books sold a million copies, so obviously the same lightning can be caught in a bottle twice.

About me: I am Emily Brontë, a social recluse who lives on the Yorkshire moors with my dog and siblings. My poetry has been self-published with little to no readers but a lot of personnel satisfaction.

Please get back to me at your earliest convenience, as this book is ready to hit the shelves as soon as possible. Time waits for no author!

Your's sincerely,

Emily Brontë

Bad Query Bingo Card

Genre mismatch: The letter opens by acknowledging the agent doesn't represent this genre but she is approaching them anyway. That's an instant delete.

Lack of proofreading: In our agent interview series, agents have mentioned that a single unfortunate typo won't sink your submission, but... there are limits.

Clichés mangled beyond repair: Best to avoid clichés, even if you get them right.

Frame device overemphasis: Brontë wastes precious space on Lockwood and Nelly rather than focusing on the central romance-and-revenge arc.

Comps issue: These are blockbuster comps, with no explanation of why she has included them beyond "those books sold a million copies." A little self-confidence is nice, but arrogance has no place in a query letter.

Word count red flag: 116k is long for a debut, and given the lack of proofreading of this query letter, agents are likely to assume the manuscript needs a sharp set of hedge shears.

Bio red flags: It's not a crime to be a private person, but someone will need to promote this book. Best to at least pretend that you're comfortable around humans. Also, "little to no readers" for her poetry collection inspires zero confidence, both in terms of craft and marketing savvy. If it happens to be true, maybe don't mention it.

Minimum effort mayhem: Overall, this query letter reads like it was hammered out in under a minute and sent without a second thought. The only thing faster will be the speed at which an agent throws it in the trash.

Take Two: The Revision

Dear Agent,

I'm seeking representation for *Wuthering Heights*, a gothic literary novel complete at 95,000 words.

When Heathcliff, an orphan raised by the Earnshaw family, falls in love with his foster sister, Catherine, their bond seems unbreakable—until she chooses to marry into wealth and social status instead. Heartbroken and furious, Heathcliff vanishes for years before returning with a fortune and a plan for vengeance that will consume not only the Earnshaws and Lintons but also the next generation, who inherit their legacy of obsession, betrayal, and grief.

Set against the wild isolation of the Yorkshire moors, *Wuthering Heights* combines gothic romance with psychological realism, exploring how love and revenge can echo through families like a curse. Comparable titles include *A House with Good Bones* by T. Kingfisher (2023), which blends ancestral curses with domestic decay; *Starling House* by Alix E. Harrow (2023), featuring a mysterious mansion, inheritance secrets, and a heroine tied to the dark history of place; and *The Bog Wife* by Kay Chronister (2024), where family, land, and hauntings overlap in both emotional and supernatural terrain.

I've previously published poetry under the pseudonym Ellis Bell in several British literary journals, and I live and work on the Yorkshire moors that inspired this story's stark setting.

Thank you for your time and consideration. I would be delighted to send the full manuscript at your request.

Sincerely,

Emily Brontë

If you were an agent and this landed on your desk...

This query lands with the right ingredients: a darkly passionate love story, family curses spanning generations, and gothic atmosphere thick enough to seep through the page. You read the pitch: love betrayed, revenge plotted, the Yorkshire moors as both stage and character. The emotional and thematic weight are clear from the start.

As an agent, you are likely to appreciate the clarity and professionalism here. The letter provides the genre, word count (yes, again, the actual novel is longer), and completion status up front, then moves efficiently into the story's arc: Heathcliff and Catherine's doomed romance, the choice that sparks his vengeance, the fallout for two families. There's a satisfying sense of shape and scope—inciting incident, escalation, and lasting consequences across generations.

The comps paragraph is solid. These titles are recent, with clear market resemblance—a signal to an agent where this novel might sit on the shelves: gothic, literary, emotionally intense, with a modern readership in mind. That positions the book well for editors looking for "literary with a strong hook" rather than purely commercial romance or pop genre.

But even with all this, a few questions linger. Gothic fiction can be a tricky sell in the current market. Readers love dark romance and psychological tension, yes—but it often needs a fresh angle or a narrative voice that grabs immediately. Agents might wonder: Does the story lean more towards literary tragedy or genre thriller? How ghastly are the ghosts in this book? Is the romance central enough for the romance market, or does it read more as literary family drama with romantic elements? And at 95,000 words, does the pacing keep the intensity high, or will readers wander the moors for too many chapters before the plot tightens?

And let's address the elephant in the room, shall we? *Falls in love with his foster sister?* That's bound to raise a few eyebrows.

Still, the query promises a bold, emotionally charged story with thematic ambition. That should be more than enough to push an agent to the sample page, where the voice and execution will either seal the deal—or not. After all, a good query will open the door, but the manuscript still has to walk through it.

Fake Query #3:
The Scarlet Letter

Overview

Nathaniel Hawthorne's *The Scarlet Letter* (1850) opens in the rigid Puritan world of seventeenth-century Boston, where Hester Prynne is publicly shamed for bearing a child out of wedlock and condemned to wear the infamous scarlet *A* on her chest for life. While the town demands repentance, Hester refuses to reveal the name of her lover, Reverend Arthur Dimmesdale, who suffers in silence as guilt consumes him. The return of Hester's long-absent husband, Roger Chillingworth, bent on revenge, drives the story towards its dark, inevitable reckoning.

Framed by a narrator in a nineteenth-century customhouse who claims to have uncovered the story's artifacts, *The Scarlet Letter* blends historical fiction with moral drama, exploring themes of sin, shame, identity, and redemption. In our Fake Deads universe, however, Hawthorne is just another hopeful author firing off a query letter to an overworked agent, trying to convince them that adultery, guilt, and Puritanism are exactly what the market needs right now.

Nathaniel Hawthorne's (Fake) Query Letter

Dear Agent,

Arising from the depths of your slush pile is my novel *The Scarlet Letter*, a work of historical fiction set in the Puritan settlement of Boston in the 1640s. It's about a woman named Hester Prynne who has an affair, gets pregnant, and is forced to wear a big red *A* for the rest of her life. As if things aren't bad enough, the town minister, Arthur Dimmesdale, turns out to be the father. He dies dramatically at the end—right after confessing in front of everyone.

Frankly, the whole publishing industry seems rigged these days. Too many gatekeepers, not enough appreciation for true literary talent. I've been in the querying trenches for months, and it's starting to feel like the Salem witch trials all over again, only with fewer torches and more form rejections.

Fans of *The Crucible* (the movie—I've never actually read the play) or *Breaking Bad* will love this story of guilt, shame, and public downfall. Like Walter White, Dimmesdale tries to hide the truth until it destroys him, though personally I think my ending is even sadder.

As for me, my self-published debut novel *Fanshawe* received several kind reviews (mainly from friends and family), though sales have been modest. Actually, I destroyed most of the unsold copies because they were taking up too much space in my barn. I also enjoy whittling, eating lobster on Tuesdays, and staring into the middle distance while thinking about sin.

I'm confident this novel will find a home with the right agent, though the odds sometimes feel worse than surviving smallpox. Thank you for your consideration, I guess.

Yours,

Nathaniel Hawthorne

Bad Query Bingo Card

Backstory overload: Hester's affair and pregnancy happen before the story starts, and then the pitch jumps right to the end. That means we don't get any sense of the narrative structure.

Reveals the ending: In a synopsis, you should reveal major twists and the ending, but a query pitch is supposed to entice. The hook won't be as sharp if the outcome is immediately revealed.

Negative tone: Querying is tough. Form rejections are tough—and nowadays authors are lucky to get even one of those. But despite the steep hill we must climb towards the promise of representation, it's not the agent's fault that the industry has become what it is. Stay positive. You are pitching a book AND a business relationship.

TV/film comps: It's not completely forbidden to use a comparable title from TV or film. Maybe there is a show or movie that perfectly fits your project. But couple that with a novel or two, otherwise the agent might wonder if you actually read.

Poor indie sales: Not all indie authors can figure out marketing, at least not with their first release. It's not a dealbreaker to have a book in the world that didn't sell into the thousands or beyond. However, it's not the strongest bullet point to include in your bio paragraph.

Odd personal trivia: Lobster Tuesdays? Whittling? On one hand, a bit of quirk in the bio can be okay. Agents are looking for capable writers whom they can also connect with, so it's not a terrible thing to express who you are. But keep it simple and professional.

Take Two: The Revision

Dear Agent,

I am seeking representation for *The Scarlet Letter*, a work of historical fiction complete at 84,000 words.

In seventeenth-century Boston, Hester Prynne is publicly condemned for adultery and forced to wear a scarlet *A* on her chest as a permanent mark of shame. Refusing to name her lover—the respected minister Arthur Dimmesdale—Hester builds a life on the edges of her Puritan community while Dimmesdale slowly deteriorates under the weight of his hidden guilt. When Hester's long-absent husband returns under a false name, determined to uncover and punish her lover, the lives of all three spiral towards a reckoning that will expose secrets, consume reputations, and test the limits of forgiveness.

The Scarlet Letter blends historical drama with themes of community, morality, and mental health, appealing to readers of *Hester* by Laurie Lico Albanese (2022) and *The House of Eve* by Sadeqa Johnson (2023)—novels that explore women's resilience, social judgment, and forbidden love in sharply realized historical settings.

I am the author of several short stories published in literary journals. My work often draws on my New England heritage and examines the lasting influence of Puritan ideals on American life and identity.

Thank you for your time and consideration. I would be delighted to send the full manuscript at your request.

Sincerely,

Nathaniel Hawthorne

If you were an agent and this landed on your desk...

Historical setting, moral complexity, a protagonist facing impossible odds. Couple that with Puritan Boston, public shaming, hidden sin and vengeance. This all sounds intriguing, and the story shape is immediately clear. That's a good start.

From an agent's perspective, several things work here. The query has a strong hook: a woman condemned in public while her lover suffers in secret and a husband plotting revenge in the shadows. There's obvious potential for conflict and drama, with stakes that blend the personal and the societal. The comps position the novel in the historical fiction market, signaling that the author knows his readership. The tone is professional and confident without spoiling the ending or overloading the query with unnecessary detail.

But some questions linger. The historical fiction market is ever-popular, but Puritan New England isn't the most in-demand period. How would this compete with stories set in more commercially attractive eras—Victorian London drama, Tudor intrigue, World War II resistance? Will the moral and religious themes feel weighty and relevant to modern readers or risk coming across as didactic and dated?

Then there's the question of pacing. The query hints at secret guilt, revenge, and eventual reckoning, but that doesn't guarantee a ton of momentum. Will the novel offer enough forward drive, or will it linger too long in interior monologues and philosophical asides?

Still, the elements of a strong story are here: scandal, repression, betrayal, and the human cost of keeping secrets. Most agents would probably request pages to see whether the execution delivers the intensity that the premise suggests.

Fake Query #4:
Anne of Green Gables

Overview

Lucy Maud Montgomery's *Anne of Green Gables* (1908) introduces readers to Anne Shirley, an imaginative, impulsive orphan mistakenly sent to live with Marilla and Matthew Cuthbert, who requested a boy to help with their farm on Prince Edward Island. Instead, they get Anne—a whirlwind of red hair, opinions, and daydreams—who promptly upends the quiet conservatism of Avonlea with her endless chatter and big personality.

As Anne stumbles through misadventures involving green hair dye, currant wine, and an academic rivalry with the infuriatingly clever Gilbert Blythe, she transforms from an unruly child into a determined young woman. The novel explores belonging, identity, and the stubborn spark of individuality set against the prim backdrop of small-town life.

But in our Fake Deads alternate universe, Montgomery is a first-time novelist armed with nothing but a query letter—one that may or may not capture the same charm as Anne herself.

Lucy Maud Montgomery's (Fake) Query Letter

Dear Most Marvelous, Glorious, Important Agent,

Oh, what a thrill to write to you! This is Anne Shirley speaking (well, through my author's hand, but really, it is *my* story). I'm positively bursting to tell you about my book, *Anne of Green Gables*, which runs to a most respectable 93,712 words because I have so many things to say, and besides, brevity is so dreadfully overrated, don't you think?

Now, where to begin? I suppose I should tell you about Matthew and Marilla Cuthbert first—they are a brother and sister who live at Green

Gables and thought they were getting a boy from the orphanage, but instead they got me, Anne-with-an-e. There's also Diana Barry, my bosom friend (she's *so* beautiful), and Gilbert Blythe, who is dreadfully annoying but also brilliant, and Mrs. Rachel Lynde, who says the most horrid things, and then there's Miss Stacy, my wonderful teacher, and several others I loathe to leave out because they're all terribly important. Anyway, I dye my hair green by mistake, get Diana drunk on currant wine (oh, the scandal!), crack my slate over Gilbert's head, and win some academic awards and whatnot. It's all really very exciting even if no one ever falls off a cliff or fights a bear or anything truly dangerous like that.

Readers who loved *The Midnight Library* or *Project Hail Mary* will simply adore this book. After all, those stories have people making big decisions and solving enormous problems, and I too make big decisions (what to wear to a tea party) and solve enormous problems (passing geometry).

As for my author, Lucy Maud Montgomery, she has always dreamed of seeing her name in the biggest possible lights, perhaps even in electric bulbs someday, which would be so glamorous. She grew up on Prince Edward Island, became very well educated indeed, and has written many poems about loneliness that really ought to have made her famous by now.

Please do read all 93,712 words at once if you can manage it. I just know you'll love my story because who wouldn't want to spend hours upon hours with me?

Yours in breathless anticipation,

Anne Shirley (and Lucy Maud Montgomery, of course)

Bad Query Bingo Card

Query in the protagonist's voice: This is something agents have mentioned to us more than once. Authors are artists. We're creative. And writing a dry business proposal doesn't feel like a lot of fun. So why not bring some of our creativity into the query letter? While we are firm believers that anything can be done well, this usually comes across as gimmicky and unprofessional.

High word count for middle grade: Times have changed. Genre and audience expectations are much more defined than they once were. For this age group, 93k words is double the expected length, which suggests the book will need editing that already should have been done.

Unnecessary repetition: In this case, the word count is mentioned twice. Sometimes in the query letters we edit, we see themes repeated, or even redundancies in the pitch. Imagine your ideal agent is up late sifting through a giant stack of submissions over a glass of wine. You want your query to read as effortlessly as possible, so short and sweet is best.

Character clutter: Don't stuff too many names into your pitch. It overwhelms the picture. Instead, focus on the core characters and conflict. Your secondary characters might be amazing, but they don't all need to make an appearance here.

Mismatched comps: *Project Hail Mary* and *The Midnight Library* have nothing to do with historical middle-grade fiction. As noted earlier, your comps represent what your future readers are reading today and should be relevant to your project in some way.

Fame-seeking bio: This bio suggests the author just wants to be famous, not build a career or reach the right readers. Sure, fame is nice, but this is a tough industry. Even for authors with agents, blockbuster success is the exception, not the rule. An agent could well be wary of a client who expects to become a household name with their debut. A bio like this is a red flag along the lines of I'M GOING TO BE DIFFICULT TO WORK WITH.

Low stakes: Hair dye, geometry exams, and tea parties don't exactly scream "must turn pages," yet there are some deeply personal stakes in this novel. The pitch just hasn't been framed in a way that makes the emotional imperative clear.

Take Two: The Revision

Dear Agent,

I am seeking representation for *Anne of Green Gables*, a middle-grade historical novel complete at 62,000 words.

When garrulous Anne Shirley arrives at Green Gables, she is not the boy Marilla and Matthew Cuthbert expected to help on their Prince Edward Island farm. Determined to prove she belongs, Anne channels her boundless imagination into winning over the skeptical villagers of

Avonlea—sometimes through charm, sometimes through chaos. From accidental hair dye disasters to fierce academic rivalries and an unexpected act of heroism, Anne's misadventures slowly transform her from a lonely orphan into a young woman who discovers family, friendship, and purpose where she least expected it.

With its blend of humour, warmth, and heartwarming stakes, *Anne of Green Gables* will appeal to readers of *The Vanderbeekers of 141st Street* by Karina Yan Glaser and *Pax* by Sara Pennypacker, middle-grade novels that explore belonging, family bonds, and the resilience of spirited young protagonists.

I grew up on Prince Edward Island, where I began writing poetry and short stories as a teenager and later studied literature and earned my teacher's licence. My deep connection to the island and its history brings authenticity to both the setting and the characters in *Anne of Green Gables*.

Thank you for your time and consideration. I would be happy to send the full manuscript at your request.

Sincerely,

Lucy Maud Montgomery

If you were an agent and this landed on your desk...

You're up late with your slush pile, and that first glass of wine has turned into a second. You open the next query, expecting yet another uninspired middle-grade submission—and instead, you find a professional, clearly written pitch with an unmistakable sense of charm. The premise is immediately clear: a feisty orphan shakes up a quiet community while finding a family of her own. The stakes aren't world-ending, but the emotional core seems strong, and the promise of humour and warmth signals a story that could win over readers of all ages.

The word count is appropriate to the readership, which reassures you this isn't a rambling manuscript that will need heavy pruning. The query focuses on Anne herself rather than listing every character in Avonlea, which gives you confidence the author knows how to centre the focus on a protagonist.

The comps do real work here too. They're recent, relevant middle-grade titles, showing the author understands the market and can picture where her novel might sit on a bookstore shelf. That's exactly what agents want to see—thoughtful positioning, not just personal inspiration.

You might still wonder about structure. Episodic novels can be tricky to sell unless the voice is irresistible or there's a strong through-line to hold it all together. But the pitch suggests a unifying arc in Anne's journey towards belonging, with key emotional milestones anchoring the story.

Bottom line: the voice in the sample pages will decide everything, but this query hints at a promising manuscript that could find a place in a competitive middle-grade market.

Fake Query #5:
Jane Eyre

Overview

Charlotte Brontë's *Jane Eyre* (1847) follows its heroine from a childhood marked by cruelty and neglect to her employment as a governess, and into a romance complicated by secrets, social class, and gothic mystery. Orphaned and unwanted, Jane grows up in the shadow of her tyrannical aunt and the grim Lowood School before taking a position at Thornfield Hall. There, she falls in love with her employer, the enigmatic Mr. Rochester, only to discover he harbours a past that could destroy them both.

The novel blends bildungsroman elements with gothic romance, moving from a story of resilience and self-respect to one of passion, morality, and personal freedom. Across this journey, Jane grapples with questions that remain startlingly modern: how to find love without losing one's independence, how to balance desire with integrity, and how to face down the metaphorical (and occasionally literal) ghosts of the past.

But of course, in the Fake Deads universe, Brontë is a first-time author showing up with an enormous manuscript and a query letter that needs to convince an agent to read the first page.

Charlotte Brontë's (Fake) Query Letter

Dear Super Important Agent,

I'm beyond thrilled to present my masterpiece of modern literature, *Jane Eyre*, a novel that is, without question, destined to dominate bestseller lists and reshape the landscape of fiction forever. At a modest 185,000 words, this sprawling epic follows my heroine Jane from her tragic orphaned childhood through her hard-won independence as a governess, all the way to her breathtaking romance with the brooding, mysterious Mr. Rochester. This is a literary tour de force that will redefine how readers experience love, morality, and gothic suspense.

The story covers everything a reader could possibly want: childhood misery, moral dilemmas, big windswept estates, mysterious laughter at night, and of course a romance so profound it will leave the entire literary world trembling. Readers will weep, they will cheer, they will send me fan mail. Truly, no contemporary work can compare to the mastery of this manuscript. I considered listing comparable titles, but frankly, there aren't any.

My target audience? Oh, everyone. Readers of all ages, from all walks of life, across every continent—this book will unite them. Whether they love romance, mystery, ghosts, or simply reading about people who walk across moors, this novel has it all.

As for me, I was homeschooled, which I'm sure explains the singular brilliance of my prose. Growing up on the Yorkshire moors gave me a sense of drama and isolation that most writers can only dream of capturing, and it shows on every page of this book.

I eagerly await your response—though I suspect you'll want to clear your schedule once you begin reading, because you will not be able to put this down.

Yours confidently,

Charlotte Brontë

Bad Query Bingo Card

Overconfidence: This author declares the novel will "dominate bestseller lists" and "reshape the landscape of fiction," leaving no room for the agent to form their own opinion. Even more, it's obnoxious. Maybe the book is good, but your dream agent probably isn't eager to work with a narcissist.

Font: Yes, indeed, this is Comic Sans. An unusual font is more likely to get you a raised eyebrow than any extra attention. Stick with the standards (Times New Roman, Arial, Calibri, Georgia).

Too long: 185,000 words for a debut = an immediate red flag. As noted elsewhere, an agent's time is very limited. Same goes for publishers. A long book takes longer to edit and prep for publication, plus the increased page count means higher printing costs, so you'll need to sell that many more books to make up the difference. That's why agents and editors aren't stoked about manuscripts that exceed 100k, especially from debut authors.

Casual, familiar tone: Phrases like "oh, everyone" and "they will send me fan mail" can undermine any sense of professionalism. While you want to come across as interesting and competent, it's important to remember this is a business proposal.

Vague audience: Claiming the book is for literally everyone is a signal the author hasn't identified a real target market.

No comps: The author refuses to list any, insisting nothing compares, which is a fairly common rookie mistake. While it's great for your book to present a fresh take, you should still have some idea who your audience will be. This bears repeating: what books are your future readers buying today?

Sprawling timeline: Agents see a lot of meandering plotlines where there isn't a tight trajectory from inciting incident to climax. While a bildungsroman does allow for an episodic structure, it's important to clarify the element that unifies the manuscript.

Homeschool mention: Not that there's anything wrong with being homeschooled, but it's an odd thing to mention in your bio as evidence that you're a fantastic writer.

Unrealistic expectations: Maybe your book will unite the globe and inspire fan mail before page one. But if an agent worries that your expectations are sky-high, they may suspect you won't be able to handle the challenges and rejection that inevitably come with the publishing industry.

Take Two: The Revision

Dear Agent,

I'm seeking representation for *Jane Eyre*, a work of historical fiction with gothic and romantic elements, complete at 98,000 words.

Orphaned as a child and raised in hardship, Jane grows up determined to claim both independence and a sense of belonging. Her position as governess at Thornfield Hall offers the promise of a new life—until she falls in love with her employer, the enigmatic Mr. Rochester, whose secrets threaten everything Jane has fought to achieve. As revelations unravel and her moral convictions collide with her longing for love, Jane must decide what she is willing to sacrifice to remain true to herself.

Jane Eyre will appeal to readers who enjoy historical fiction with a supernatural edge and strong romantic arcs. Comparable titles include *The Bog Wife* by Kay Chronister (2024), which weaves family secrets and Southern gothic dread into a deeply atmospheric setting; *A House with Good Bones* by T. Kingfisher (2023), with its emotional family legacies and haunted home as a character; and *Midnight Rooms* by Donyae Coles (2024), a gothic romantasy that bleeds into mystery and darkness.

I grew up in the Yorkshire countryside, where the isolation and drama of the moors shaped my writing as much as my early passion for literature. My work has appeared in local periodicals, and *Jane Eyre* marks my debut in historical fiction.

Thank you for your time and consideration. I would be delighted to send the full manuscript at your request.

Sincerely,

Charlotte Brontë

If you were an agent and this landed on your desk...

It's Monday morning. Your inbox is overflowing, and your caffeine levels are dropping. You open a query for a debut historical novel called *Jane Eyre*. At first glance, it looks promising. The word count is a reasonable 98k words, the pitch offers gothic mystery wrapped around a romantic core, and the protagonist has both drive and moral conflict. You can see the narrative spine: an orphan who becomes a governess, a love affair complicated by secrets, a heroine forced to choose between passion and principle. That's a solid setup for character development and emotional draw.

But you're also weighing the market. Historical fiction with a gothic edge continues to sell well, especially when blended with romance, so the comps reinforce the market appeal. They're recent, they signal tone and audience, and they tell you this author knows her market. You're not looking at someone who thinks they've invented literature itself.

Still, you'd probably ask a few questions before getting too excited. How much of Jane's early years make it onto the page? Episodic historical fiction can sometimes drift without clear momentum, and you'll want to be sure *Jane Eyre* avoids that trap. Is the romance central enough to carry the plot? Will the gothic elements lean into suspense or just create atmosphere? And how does the balance between love story and moral reckoning play out in the end?

All of this means you're likely heading straight to the sample pages. The query provides plenty of reasons to get excited. Fingers crossed that the writing will deliver on its promise. Whether you request the full manuscript will depend on how the first paragraph, first page, and first chapter land.

Part Two: Fake Synopses

What Makes a Good Synopsis?

When an agent requests a synopsis as part of their submission requirements, they're looking to gauge the manuscript's narrative structure. As F. Scott Fitzgerald said, "Plot is character, character is plot." In other words, agents want to see evidence of a strong plot (which means each development is connected by causality), a unique and compelling protagonist (or more than one), and a solid story arc (the intersection of the protagonist's internal and external conflicts, resulting in a transformation of some kind). You don't have room in a synopsis for much detail. What you're providing here are the broad brushstrokes of your novel: the main characters, key plot elements, and central trajectory.

As for length, some agents will ask for a synopsis of about 500 words, while others are open to 1000 words—but rarely longer than that. For our (fake) synopses, we've stuck to under 500 words to demonstrate that even structurally complex classics can be summarized succinctly by zooming in on the most important elements. Many of the synopses that clients send us are overstuffed with characters and subplots that don't necessarily need to be included.

One thing you do want to do in a synopsis is tell the whole story from start to finish. An agent wants to assess whether you can get a story off the ground and land it again at the end.

Let's return to our five chosen classics and see how these authors might have handled their synopses.

Fake Synopsis #1: Pride and Prejudice

In Regency England, ELIZABETH BENNET lives in the household of MR. BENNET and MRS. BENNET with sisters JANE BENNET, LYDIA BENNET, KITTY BENNET, and MARY BENNET. MRS. BENNET identifies marriage as the primary objective for daughters. MR. BENNET demonstrates passive resistance to this objective but contributes no alternate plan.

Arrival of MR. CHARLES BINGLEY at Netherfield Park initiates sequence of social interactions. MR. BINGLEY arrives with sisters CAROLINE BINGLEY and MRS. LOUISA HURST, plus associate MR. FITZWILLIAM DARCY. At initial dance event, MR. DARCY rejects ELIZABETH BENNET as a potential partner. ELIZABETH BENNET records negative assessment of MR. DARCY based on overheard comment.

MR. BINGLEY exhibits preference for JANE BENNET. MRS. BENNET reports this development to neighbours repeatedly. MARY BENNET performs on the piano without audience request. LYDIA BENNET and KITTY BENNET observe militia units in Meryton. They meet MR. GEORGE WICKHAM, who reports negative history with MR. DARCY, producing additional bias in ELIZABETH BENNET against MR. DARCY.

MR. COLLINS, identified as heir to the Bennet estate, arrives with intention to marry one Bennet daughter to mitigate inheritance transfer issues. He proposes to ELIZABETH BENNET following limited conversation. Proposal rejected. MR. COLLINS immediately redirects proposal to CHARLOTTE LUCAS. Acceptance occurs with no observed romantic basis.

ELIZABETH BENNET visits CHARLOTTE LUCAS and MR. COLLINS at Hunsford Parsonage. Proximity to LADY CATHERINE DE BOURGH results in repeated lectures from LADY CATHERINE DE BOURGH regarding ELIZABETH BENNET's deficiencies.

MR. DARCY proposes to ELIZABETH BENNET without prior emotional calibration. Proposal references ELIZABETH BENNET's inferior social position. Rejection issued. ELIZABETH BENNET accuses MR. DARCY of sabotaging JANE BENNET–MR. BINGLEY relationship and mistreating MR. WICKHAM. MR. DARCY supplies written document contradicting MR. WICKHAM's claims and providing alternate narrative involving GEORGIANA DARCY elopement attempt.

ELIZABETH BENNET visits Pemberley estate with MR. and MRS. GARDINER. Observations indicate MR. DARCY maintains positive relationships with staff and GEORGIANA DARCY.

LYDIA BENNET elopes with MR. WICKHAM. Family reputation experiences degradation risk. MR. BENNET travels without success. MRS. BENNET expresses high distress. MARY BENNET plays piano again. KITTY BENNET cries. Resolution achieved when MR. DARCY provides financial settlement compelling MR. WICKHAM to marry LYDIA BENNET.

MR. BINGLEY resumes courtship of JANE BENNET. Engagement follows. LADY CATHERINE DE BOURGH confronts ELIZABETH BENNET to prevent MR. DARCY marriage proposal. ELIZABETH BENNET refuses compliance. MR. DARCY proposes again. Acceptance issued.

Terminal status: JANE BENNET marries MR. BINGLEY. ELIZABETH BENNET marries MR. DARCY. LYDIA BENNET and MR. WICKHAM maintain unstable marriage. CHARLOTTE LUCAS and MR. COLLINS persist in practicality. KITTY BENNET improves via married sisters. MARY BENNET continues piano.

Syn Sins

When it comes to crafting a synopsis, there are a lot of deadly sins that might tempt you—but resist them if you can. Poor Ms. Austen has succumbed to several:

Too many characters: Limited word count means you simply can't include every character in the novel. Keep it simple and stick to the main ones. And assume the reader can remember last names: the Bennet-Bennet-Bennet-ness of this synopsis is both exhausting and unnecessary. Also note that character names need only be capitalized the first time they're mentioned.

Too many subplots: The main storyline is what an agent wants to see: Does it hang together? Does it make sense? Is it compelling? As soon as you start introducing subplots, you risk both confusion and overwhelm. A synopsis that includes too many plot points sounds like a grocery list of events that aren't connected by causality.

Too busy in general: The level of detail in this synopsis feels like one of those closets crammed with tennis racquets, winter coats, and the skis no one uses anymore. Minimize. Take a page out of Marie Kondo's book and only keep what will spark joy for an agent.

Robotic voice: Is it hard to describe a novel in 500 words? Sure. But that doesn't mean you should do it in Morse code. While this synopsis is an exaggerated example, the tendency to cram can cause odd word choices, clunky phrasing, and missed words. If in doubt, read your synopsis out loud—either to yourself, or better yet, to a friend who hasn't read your book. If they're confused, or if you sound like Robot Jane, rewrite it until it's smooth. It will save you a slew of delete-rejections.

Take Two: The Revision

In the quiet countryside of Regency England, the Bennet household hums with both charm and anxiety. MRS. BENNET, ever mindful of her five daughters' unmarried status, dreams of advantageous matches, while MR. BENNET watches his wife's matchmaking schemes with dry amusement.

When a wealthy bachelor, MR. BINGLEY, leases nearby Netherfield Park, news spreads quickly. At the ball he puts on, his friendly manner delights everyone—especially the eldest daughter, JANE BENNET, whose gentle beauty captures his admiration. His friend, the reserved and proud MR. DARCY, makes a colder impression, dismissing ELIZABETH BENNET with cutting remarks she is not meant to overhear. Elizabeth, spirited and quick-witted, forms an immediate dislike for the man, setting the stage for a clash of tempers and pride.

As Jane and Bingley's romance blooms, the militia arrives, bringing with it the charming MR. WICKHAM. Elizabeth is drawn to his easy manner and his account of being wronged by Mr. Darcy. Each word Wickham speaks seems to confirm her first impression: Darcy is arrogant, heartless, and undeserving of sympathy.

The story twists when MR. COLLINS, the pompous heir to the Bennet estate, proposes to Elizabeth after only a few days' acquaintance. Her refusal scandalizes her mother, but Mr. Collins recovers quickly by proposing to CHARLOTTE LUCAS, Elizabeth's sensible friend, who accepts for financial security rather than love. Unbeknownst to Elizabeth, Mr. Darcy and Bingley's sisters convince Bingley that Jane doesn't care for him, causing him to leave Netherfield Park with them.

Visiting Charlotte at her new home, Elizabeth encounters Mr. Darcy again at nearby Rosings Park. To her astonishment, he confesses his love and proposes—awkwardly, with a blunt reminder of her inferior connections. Offended, Elizabeth refuses him, accusing him of destroying Jane and Bingley's happiness and mistreating Wickham.

Darcy's letter the next day shatters her certainty. He reveals Wickham's betrayal and his true motives for separating Jane and Bingley: he believed Jane indifferent. Elizabeth begins to question not only Darcy's character but also her own judgment.

Months later, visiting Darcy's grand estate at Pemberley, Elizabeth hears accounts of his generosity and witnesses his warmth towards his sister. Just as her feelings begin to change, LYDIA, the youngest Bennet sister, elopes with Wickham, threatening the family's honour. Elizabeth later learns that Darcy has intervened, arranging their marriage and saving her family from ruin.

Bingley soon returns to propose to Jane, while Darcy, humbled and hopeful, asks Elizabeth once more. This time, with pride set aside and prejudices dissolved, she accepts.

Through wit, romance, and social drama, *Pride and Prejudice* traces the journey from first impressions to lasting love, where self-knowledge proves the truest victory.

If you were an agent and this landed on your desk...

What would be your impression of the story? Is this something you think might appeal to readers? Would you turn to the writing sample? If so, why? What catches your attention?

Strengths: There's lots of intrigue to recommend this story. The issue of marrying for happiness versus financial security was a genuine concern for a woman at that time, and the situation seems ripe for social commentary. The story promises to be more than a mere romp through bedrooms and ballrooms.

As well, the lively cast of characters sounds multifaceted and complex, with internal conflicts that will help them come alive on the page and create connection with the reader. The structure seems sound and under control.

Snags: Five sisters are a lot to keep track of. Are they all necessary? Do they each pull their weight? Are they differentiated enough to justify keeping them? This might be something that raises an agent's eyebrow.

Overall: This is no debut. Austen has a strong track record, and that goes a long way with an agent. Regardless of the possible snags, most agents would be inclined to look at the writing sample and see how the author's new manuscript stands up to her previous one.

Fake Synopsis #2: Wuthering Heights

Long ago, before the true events even begin, a noble and terribly misunderstood narrator, MR. LOCKWOOD, finds himself ensnared—nay, embroiled—in the vast, labyrinthine history of Wuthering Heights. His letters, each more revealing than the last, draw upon the reminiscences of NELLY DEAN, the faithful housekeeper, who spares no words—absolutely none—in laying out the comprehensive lineage, genealogy, and backstory of every inhabitant who so much as looked at the Heights in passing.

Through these endless recollections emerges the tragic and soaring tale of HEATHCLIFF, the darkly tempestuous orphan whose passions run as wild as the gales upon the Yorkshire moors. Adopted by the benevolent MR. EARNSHAW yet scorned by the cruel HINDLEY, Heathcliff grows up alongside the ethereal CATHERINE, whose soul seems bound to his by cosmic threads of fate, time, and perhaps metaphysical destiny itself. They run wild upon the heath, swearing eternal devotion, and though Catherine is technically his foster sister—well, the heart, dear reader, cannot be confined by mere propriety, and their love blooms like a windswept rose upon a lonely crag.

Alas! Catherine, desiring social elevation and perhaps finer curtains, weds the well-mannered EDGAR LINTON, leaving Heathcliff to depart in mysterious rage, only to return years later enriched, embittered, and bent upon a revenge that will transcend generations. With Byronic intensity, he dismantles Hindley's fortune, degrades young HARETON (Hindley's hapless son), ensnares ISABELLA LINTON in a loveless marriage, and schemes relentlessly to wed the fragile LINTON HEATHCLIFF—his own sickly progeny—to the innocent young CATHY, daughter of Edgar and Catherine, thereby uniting the estates of Wuthering Heights and Thrushcross Grange under his vengeful dominion.

Ghosts howl upon the moors. Tea is served, though bitterly. Inheritance documents change hands with alarming frequency. Heathcliff, consumed by passions infernal and eternal, stalks the corridors at night, believing himself haunted by Catherine's spectre—or perhaps by his own inexorable longing. The younger generation trembles before his wrath even as they unknowingly enact a slow, redemptive counterpoint to the tragedies of their elders.

What becomes of these hapless heirs? Do love and forgiveness conquer rage and retribution? Or do the sins of the fathers—and mothers, and guardians, and tenants—doom them to endless suffering beneath the pitiless winds of fate? The tale concludes—or does it?—upon a note as mysterious and untamed as the moors themselves.

Syn Sins

When it sounds like writing: Elmore Leonard had a foolproof cure for overly flowery prose: do everyone a favour and cut it. You only have 500 words. Don't waste them on prose that doesn't serve your purpose—which in this case is clarity of structure.

Romance with a foster sibling (LOLWUT?): Life on the moors gets weird fast. Heathcliff arrives as a stray kid, and though not a blood relative, the shared childhood still tangles the romance in ways that may raise modern eyebrows.

End left ambiguous: A synopsis is not a back-jacket blurb. Your job here is to tell the whole story from start to finish. The point behind a synopsis is to demonstrate that your story hangs together, that it's cohesive and logical and that you've pulled it off. If you leave the ending out, it doesn't reassure the agent. They might worry that you've done this either because you don't know how it ends or you do know—and you know you haven't landed it well. Either way, they worry, and a worried agent is an agent who tends to say *no*.

Too much backstory at the beginning: Yes, you want to supply context so the agent has a sense of where and when this story will unfold, but don't waste precious space on backstory. Even here, keep your reader on a need-to-know basis. Give us the bare minimum and then get on with it.

Speaking of TMI: While the structure of the frame is important to *Wuthering Heights*, all an agent really needs to know is that it exists. Spending all that time describing the frame might make the agent think the story itself is thin and the author is struggling.

Take Two: The Revision

When MR. LOCKWOOD leases Thrushcross Grange, seeking peace on the Yorkshire moors, he instead encounters the brooding master of Wuthering Heights, HEATHCLIFF—a man whose bitterness seems carved into the land itself. Intrigued, Lockwood presses the housekeeper, NELLY DEAN, for the tale behind her enigmatic employer.

Years earlier, MR. EARNSHAW brought home a dark, ragged foundling from Liverpool, raising him alongside his own children, HINDLEY and CATHERINE. While Catherine forms an unshakable bond with the boy she calls Heathcliff, Hindley grows resentful, jealousy hardening into cruelty after their father's death. Reduced to a servant under Hindley's rule, Heathcliff burns with humiliation—and a fierce, unyielding love for Catherine.

But Catherine, longing for social respectability, chooses marriage to EDGAR LINTON of Thrushcross Grange. Her decision shatters Heathcliff. He disappears, only to return years later transformed—educated, wealthy, and driven by a singular purpose: revenge.

Heathcliff methodically acquires Wuthering Heights from a ruined Hindley, takes control of Thrushcross Grange by arranging the sickly LINTON HEATHCLIFF's marriage to young CATHERINE LINTON (Catherine and Edgar's daughter), and degrades HARETON, Hindley's son, reducing him to the illiteracy and coarseness once inflicted upon him. Yet triumph brings him no peace. Catherine's death leaves Heathcliff haunted, her memory a torment he both clings to and rails against.

As years pass, the younger generation—Cathy Linton, Linton Heathcliff, and Hareton Earnshaw—become entangled in the legacy of bitterness Heathcliff has engineered. Linton dies after his coerced marriage to Cathy, leaving Heathcliff master of both houses. Yet Cathy's growing bond with Hareton thaws some of the hatred rooted in the Heights.

In his final days, Heathcliff is consumed by visions of Catherine, convinced her spirit waits for him on the moors. He stops eating, stops scheming, and finally dies, buried beside the woman whose love and loss shaped his life.

With Heathcliff gone, Cathy and Hareton plan a future together, their relationship a quiet counterpoint to the violence and obsession that dominated the previous generation. The cycle of vengeance ends, leaving the moors—and the families who endure there—changed but not destroyed.

If you were an agent and this landed on your desk...

Would you eagerly turn to the sample pages? If so, why? If not, what makes you hesitate?

Strengths: This synopsis starts with setting, which leads us to believe the setting will play a significant role. Brontë mentioned the landscape in her bio, so this could be a great strength of the novel and provide a solid foundation for the story as well as contribute to an overall creepy and haunting vibe.

Family is always fertile ground for conflict, and an agent might be intrigued by the idea that it's not just wealth that can be passed on from one generation to the next but also hatred and rivalry. The theme is timeless. Heathcliff comes across as a strong antihero bent on revenge. His goal is clear; his motivation is persuasive. The plot makes logical sense and feels causal. We get a sense of building momentum even in this one-page summary. (And by the way, if your synopsis is nothing but a series of *and then*s, that's a red flag that your plot doesn't have the cohesion that it needs.)

Snags: What exactly does Mr. Lockwood do in this novel? Why has the author chosen him of all people to frame it? Is this frame structure even necessary? Leaving that aside, we can't ignore that eyebrow-raising relationship between foster siblings, and depending on the agent, that could be a make-or-break issue.

Overall: The power of the landscape combined with the potentially explosive emotions make this sound like a submission worth reading. We would have to see how Brontë handles the narration, but based on this synopsis, it seems worth taking the plunge.

Fake Synopsis #3: The Scarlet Letter

In the strict, buttoned-up town of Boston, during the super-fun Puritan era, there's this woman named HESTER PRYNNE who shows up from overseas. She's supposed to be waiting for her husband, but—surprise!—he never shows. Left alone in a town where people are way too obsessed with moral righteousness, Hester ends up in a bit of a scandal by falling for another guy. One thing leads to another, and bam, she has a baby, PEARL. The town? Not so thrilled. Also not thrilled: the town leaders, who don't just see a baby, but a walking, cooing embodiment of sin. Symbolism alert.

As punishment, Hester gets slapped with the scarlet letter *A* for "adulteress," which she has to wear like a permanent fashion accessory. But instead of making it dull and sad, Hester, being a total badass, embroiders it all fancy, turning her shame into a statement piece. The Puritans don't appreciate the irony, but anyone paying attention can see this is obviously about rebellion, individuality, and maybe proto-feminism centuries before that was even a thing. The town forces her to stand on a scaffold, holding little Pearl, while everyone watches and judges. Enter ARTHUR DIMMESDALE, the town's beloved preacher, who asks her to reveal who the baby daddy is. No chance—Hester is keeping that secret. But plot twist: the real baby daddy is Dimmesdale himself, though only one other person besides Hester knows it. That other person? A walking, talking symbol of vengeance who arrives on cue.

That would be ROGER CHILLINGWORTH, Hester's long-lost (and presumed dead) husband, who just so happens to show up in Boston on the exact day of her public shaming. Symbolism practically drips off this coincidence, like fate itself is arranging for maximum drama. He's not thrilled, to say the least. He swears to find out who knocked up his wife and sets his sights on Dimmesdale, pretending to be a friendly physician while actually slowly tormenting the poor guy, who's already losing it from guilt—a guilt that clearly represents inner doubt and spiritual decay, in case the name Dimmesdale wasn't enough of a hint.

Over time, Hester patches things up by working hard and minding her own business. The scarlet letter, once a red flag (literally), eventually becomes something people in town kind of respect—because society loves irony almost as much as symbolism. But while Hester's street cred improves,

Dimmesdale spirals into guilt-driven misery, and Chillingworth gets even creepier in his quest for revenge, his name basically underlining his cold-blooded malice in all caps.

Everything comes to a head when Dimmesdale, too messed up to handle his secret any longer, decides to spill the beans. He confesses his sin in front of everyone, right on the same scaffold where Hester stood years earlier (more symbolism, obviously). Then he randomly dies, but at least he's now at peace with his maker, leaving Hester and Pearl to figure out what's next for their weird little family, possibly while serving as metaphors for grace, resilience, and new beginnings.

Syn Sins

Huge tone mismatch: This is a historical novel, and yet the synopsis reads like the description of a Netflix series. An agent might worry that this is the extent of the author's range because they Just. Don't. Read.

Reliance on coincidence: The husband *happens* to show up? Hmm. While Pixar's rule is worth mentioning—a coincidence that gets the main character into trouble is acceptable, whereas one that gets them out of trouble is not—any coincidence can hoist a red flag in an agent's mind. Coincidences take agency away from the protagonist. They're usually the easy (dare we say lazy?) way out.

Too much backstory: An agent needs to know that you can tell a story from start to finish. What they don't need to know is all the background information before the story gets started. You don't want your synopsis to double as a sleep aid.

Editorializing about the symbolism: If you have to point out the symbols, they either aren't working or you don't trust your reader. Symbols don't belong in a synopsis anyway. They should be quietly doing their work in the novel so that English teachers have something to talk about when their class studies your book.

Take Two: The Revision

In seventeenth-century Boston, during the height of Puritan rule, HESTER PRYNNE arrives from England to await her husband, who has yet to join her in the New World. Time passes. No husband comes. Alone in a rigid, judgemental community, Hester seeks solace and love elsewhere—and bears a child, PEARL, out of wedlock. Her pregnancy exposes her secret to the entire town, which responds with swift and merciless punishment: she must wear a scarlet *A* on her chest for the rest of her life, a permanent symbol of adultery and shame.

The story opens with Hester on the public scaffold, cradling Pearl as the townspeople watch in grim silence. ARTHUR DIMMESDALE, the young minister, beloved for his piety, urges her to reveal the name of the child's father—Dimmesdale himself. Hester refuses, protecting him even as she bears the full weight of the community's condemnation. Only one other man knows the truth: ROGER CHILLINGWORTH, Hester's long-absent husband, whose sudden arrival feels like fate tightening its grip. Under a false name, Chillingworth vows revenge—not on Hester, but on the unknown man who betrayed him.

As Hester rebuilds her life on the margins of society, she transforms the scarlet letter through quiet defiance. She embroiders it with gold thread. She works tirelessly as a seamstress. Over time, the townspeople read new meaning in the letter, interpreting it as "Able" rather than "Adulteress," though Hester herself never escapes its weight. Meanwhile, Dimmesdale, wracked by guilt and secrecy, deteriorates under Chillingworth's calculated psychological torment. Posing as a caring physician, Chillingworth exploits Dimmesdale's weakness, feeding his paranoia and despair in the hope of breaking him completely.

Years pass. Pearl grows. Hester endures. Dimmesdale withers beneath his conscience and Chillingworth's relentless need for vengeance. At last, unable to bear the burden any longer, Dimmesdale ascends the same scaffold where Hester once stood. In a final act of confession, he reveals himself as Pearl's father before the entire town. The effort costs him his life. He dies in Hester's arms, freed at last from secrecy and shame.

Chillingworth, robbed of his revenge, withers and dies soon after, leaving Pearl a substantial inheritance. Hester and Pearl leave Boston for many years; when Hester finally returns alone, she resumes wearing the scarlet letter by choice. She lives out her days quietly, a woman shaped but not broken by love, sin, and judgement, until she is buried near Dimmesdale, their graves marked by a single red *A*.

If you were an agent and this landed on your desk...

Would this synopsis compel you to turn to the opening pages, or would you consign it to the round file?

Strengths: What's working well here are the three main characters: Hester, Dimmesdale, and Chillingworth. Each has a clear, specific, and relatable motivation, along with an arc that promises to be satisfying. Hawthorne begins the synopsis with a short bit of context—just enough to situate us in the story. He doesn't overwhelm us with details that we don't need.

Snags: That coincidence of Chillingworth appearing at just the right time still irks us. An agent might be able to overlook it, but that could be a subjective call depending on how they feel about the device.

Overall: Most agents, regardless of the synopsis and query letter, will take at least a passing glance at the opening pages. This synopsis does have some things to recommend it: a sound structure, a solid historical foundation based on the author's knowledge, and a rich emotional landscape. Still, the writing sample will have to do some significant heavy lifting to convince us to ask for the whole manuscript.

Fake Synopsis #4: Anne of Green Gables

I arrive in Avonlea feeling both nervous and thrilled. But when I step off the train, my new adoptive father says to me, "Oh! You can talk as much as you like. I don't mind." What a relief. I know we are going to get along together just fine. So I stretch my arms wide and declare, "Dear old world. You are very lovely, and I am glad to be alive in you." I have red hair, freckles, a wild imagination—and I am determined to make Green Gables my home.

So it turns out that my new parents, MARILLA and MATTHEW CUTHBERT (an elderly brother and sister, and not a married couple as you might expect), wanted a boy to help with the farm. They got me instead. At first Marilla insists I must be sent away. But Matthew looks at me kindly, and somehow I charm Marilla with my talk, my mistakes, and my very loud heart.

Days pass in sparkling stories: I accidentally dye my hair green. I break a slate over GILBERT BLYTHE's head when he teases me by calling me "Carrots." At one point, I'm forced to confess: "People laugh at me because I use big words. But if you have big ideas, you have to use big words to express them, haven't you?" That earns some groans, but I like it anyway. At school I win top marks in spelling and more—thrill of applause! At night I stare out windows and dream of what might happen tomorrow.

I giggle, I cry, I write letters. Best friend DIANA BARRY becomes my kindred spirit. I wander by brooks, I pick daisies, I imagine everything beautiful possible. I marvel at every sunrise and autumn leaf, as though nature itself is singing just for me.

But life is not just joyful misadventures. Matthew becomes sick and one morning does not wake. My heart properly breaks in two. Marilla's eyes grow dim; the chores multiply; the farm needs help. And so I face a choice: leave Avonlea to accept a scholarship and study elsewhere, or stay to care for Marilla and the place that has become home. But of course I choose the latter. I take a teaching position locally, setting aside dreams of distant schoolrooms, because home is filled with too much love to leave.

Still, I carry hope. I learn that there are some things I can't control: death, dumb mistakes, moments when imagination fails. But I also learn that kindness, loyalty, and creativity matter more than being anywhere grand.

At the end, I walk through the fields by Green Gables, breathing in wind and light. I think: "It's not what the world holds for you. It's what you bring to it." I stay. I teach. I love. I forgive life's cruelties. And in this small world I build something soft and strong.

Syn Sins

Quotes/dialogue incorporated from the book: Seems like a good idea. Usually it isn't. Your limited space is better spent rounding out the structure of the story. In this case, the author has shoehorned the quotes into the synopsis in a way that makes them feel awkward and clunky.

First person, present tense: Even if the novel is in first person, present tense, we would advise against writing the synopsis this way. This is a business document. Writing it in this style makes it feel like you've used pink paper and covered it with unicorn stickers. (Don't do those things either, not even to make your work stand out. It will, but not in the way you're hoping.)

Speaking of first person: Unless you're very careful, you will create the I, I, I effect, as the author has done here. If you're not sure what we mean, read this synopsis out loud.

Focus is on the episodic rather than the arc: We've said it often now, but based on the many synopses we've read, it bears repeating: the point of this document is to show the entire arc of the novel from start to finish because an agent wants to see if there is one and if it's sound. This is what can make a synopsis so heartless: that moment when you try to write it and discover there isn't an arc, so you do something like this instead. Or you mistake the episodic for an arc, which will only get you a slew of rejections. Either way, it isn't working.

Uncertain readership: This is something that should be made clear in the query letter, but even here in the synopsis it's unclear who the author intends as her readers. The tone suggests a young audience, but the range of the protagonist's experience suggests an older one. What this transmits to an agent is a book that suffers from an identity crisis.

Low stakes: Stakes are essential in a novel, and an agent needs to know what they are. If very little is at stake, the reader will find lots of more interesting things to do than read your book. We will not be on the edge of our seat just because your character knows how to use big words.

Take Two: The Revision

In the rolling fields of Prince Edward Island, ageing siblings MARILLA and MATTHEW CUTHBERT set out to adopt a boy to help with farmwork at Green Gables. But when a spirited red-haired girl named ANNE SHIRLEY arrives instead, their plans—and their lives—change in ways they never imagined. From the moment Anne steps off the train, brimming with imagination and chatter, she captures Matthew's gentle heart. Marilla, practical and no-nonsense, resolves at first to send Anne back but soon finds herself drawn in by the girl's fierce intelligence, humour, and desire for belonging.

Anne throws herself into life at Green Gables with unrestrained enthusiasm. Her misadventures become legend in Avonlea: accidentally serving currant wine to her best friend DIANA BARRY instead of raspberry cordial, smashing a slate over GILBERT BLYTHE's head after he calls her "Carrots," and dyeing her hair green in a fit of vanity gone wrong. These escapades, both comic and touching, slowly win over even the most skeptical neighbours. Underneath the chaos lies Anne's determination to prove herself worthy of the home she has found.

At school, Anne's quick wit and academic ambition ignite a fierce rivalry with Gilbert, whose teasing belies a growing admiration. Their competition pushes Anne to excel, and her dedication earns her a prestigious scholarship for further studies. Yet ambition never eclipses her wonder at the world around her. She finds joy in simple beauty, loyalty in friendship, and comfort in the love slowly blossoming at Green Gables.

But life brings shadows as well as sunlight. When Matthew dies suddenly of a heart attack, Anne's triumphs pale beside the grief of losing the man who quietly became her anchor. With Marilla's eyesight failing and the farm in need of care, Anne makes the selfless choice to give up her scholarship and remain in Avonlea. She accepts a local teaching post, determined to support the woman who gave her a home when no one else would.

As Anne stands on the familiar ridge above Green Gables, she reflects on the path that brought her here—from unwanted orphan to beloved daughter, loyal friend, and determined young woman. Her dreams have changed shape, but not direction; she still longs to better the world around her, starting with the small corner she calls home.

Anne Shirley brings imagination, courage, and love to every life she touches, proving that even the quietest places can hold the widest worlds.

If you were an agent and this landed on your desk...

How would you respond to this synopsis? Does it sound like something that might make a good novel, or would it send most readers back to their Instagram feed?

Strengths: Anne Shirley's character seems like it will drive the plot—indeed, it will create the plot—and that bodes well. If a reader connects with the protagonist, they become invested emotionally in the story and will follow them anywhere. Strong characterization is essential to a good story, and this synopsis suggests that Montgomery has the right instincts for that.

Not only do we meet a compelling character, but we also see evidence of her transformation. She won't be boring.

The synopsis suggests there will be humour in the story, but also poignancy. With Matthew's death, Anne will face a tough decision that proves the worth of her character—and we suspect readers will love her for it.

Snags: There might still be some concern over who the reader will be for this book given the time span of the narrative, but this is something that can be determined in the manuscript itself.

Overall: This is an effective synopsis that hits all the key structural points, suggesting that this author understands how to write a novel. Anne starts off with a convincing motivation: to persuade the Cuthberts to keep her. Her journey builds towards a false victory with her scholarship, followed by a tragic climax that further cements her strong character and hard-won maturity. The writing sample should give us a clear indication of whether the author can deliver on these promises, so we would certainly turn to the opening pages based on this summary.

What about you?

Fake Synopsis #5: Jane Eyre

What does it mean to truly be independent? And how can a woman in nineteenth-century England reconcile autonomy, morality, and love? Jane Eyre asks these questions across a sweeping narrative that belongs firmly in the tradition of the bildungsroman—a term often misunderstood. While "coming-of-age" stories emphasize youth and innocence giving way to experience, a bildungsroman can take place over a longer period of time and concerns itself more with the inner life: the moral, intellectual, and spiritual growth of the protagonist. In *Jane Eyre*, this distinction is crucial, for the novel never stops interrogating the moral dimensions of selfhood.

The novel proceeds in two broad movements, each rich with thematic gravitas:

- **The Education of Jane**: Orphaned and mistreated at Gateshead Hall, Jane learns the coldness of social hierarchies. At Lowood School, amid deprivation and disease, she absorbs both Christian endurance and a proto-feminist sense of injustice.
- **The Temptations of the Heart**: At Thornfield Hall, where she becomes a governess, Jane encounters not only the enigmatic Mr. Rochester but also the gothic itself—secrets in attics, strange noises, a mysterious fire.

Here the narrative lingers on motifs of passion and restraint, as though the plot exists merely to give shape to theme. Jane's story unfolds as much through ideas as through events:

- **Autonomy Versus Desire**: Can a woman pursue love without surrendering her self-respect?
- **Morality Versus Happiness**: What is the cost of adhering to one's principles in the face of loneliness?
- **Society Versus the Soul**: How can spiritual equality exist within patriarchal structures?

As Jane discovers Rochester's secret—a mad wife hidden away—the text pivots not towards sensationalism but inward, exploring how betrayal and longing collide within a single conscience.

Financial independence arrives for Jane suddenly, through an inheritance rather than ambition, underscoring how material freedom enables moral choice. Yet the novel pointedly refuses to reduce her to mere romantic destiny. Each of her decisions orbits the text's central preoccupation: What does it mean to live with integrity? When the zealous St. John Rivers proposes a loveless marriage, the question is not only whether Jane will accept but also what acceptance would mean for her moral autonomy.

The ending invites readers to consider whether marriage, passion, and independence can truly coexist—or whether compromise is inevitable when ideals meet reality.

Is *Jane Eyre* ultimately a love story, a feminist treatise, or a spiritual allegory? Read on, dear agent, to find out for yourself.

Syn Sins

Focus is on theme more than plot: Mentioning the themes in a synopsis? Sure. Fixating on them at the expense of the story's structure? No. This synopsis will make an agent suspect that Charlotte Brontë either doesn't have a story or doesn't know how to tell one. *Tell* being the operative word here, because it sounds like the novel will be more like a treatise.

Ending left out: This is such a common sin we've committed it twice. Don't leave an agent in suspense. That's a back-jacket's job. A synopsis must reveal the entire story from start to finish so an agent can see if it will work. And don't end with a question. In a synopsis, the questions at the end should have answers.

Using bullet points: Maybe this seems like a good way to maximize your 500 words, but bullet points make a synopsis feel disjointed, more like a dry list of facts than a smooth summary of your story.

Explaining the bildungsroman: No one likes being lectured to. Assume an agent has access to the internet and knows how to look up unfamiliar words. Better yet, save these sorts of classifications for your query letter, where they belong.

Take Two: The Revision

From the isolated moors of northern England comes the story of JANE EYRE, a heroine whose quest for love and independence unfolds amidst mystery, passion, and betrayal. Told in her own voice, the novel follows Jane from an unloved childhood to a life shaped by choices that defy convention.

Orphaned and despised by her relatives at Gateshead Hall, Jane grows up under constant humiliation. Yet the harshness of her early years forges an unshakable resolve. At Lowood School, where privation and cruelty rule, she endures suffering but discovers friendship, intellect, and faith in her own principles. By the time she leaves to work as a governess, she carries with her both scars and strength.

Thornfield Hall offers a new beginning—and an enigma. EDWARD ROCHESTER, her employer, is mercurial, fascinating, and marked by shadows Jane cannot yet name. Their relationship grows through wit and candor into a love that threatens to upend Jane's hard-won independence. When Rochester proposes, she accepts, believing happiness finally within reach—until the wedding day reveals his secret: a wife, BERTHA MASON, alive yet hidden, driven to madness and locked away in Thornfield's attic.

Jane refuses to become Rochester's mistress. Fleeing into poverty rather than compromising her integrity, she is taken in by the Rivers family, where unexpected kinship and a surprise inheritance grant her both stability and wealth. Yet duty threatens to cage her once more when ST. JOHN RIVERS, austere and self-denying, proposes a loveless marriage for the sake of missionary work abroad.

Haunted by memories of Rochester, Jane goes back—only to find Thornfield burned, Bertha dead by her own hand, and Rochester maimed and blinded in the fire. Their reunion at Ferndean unfolds not as savior and saved, but as equals remade by suffering and loss. Jane marries him freely, fortune and independence intact, her choice rooted in respect as much as love.

Jane Eyre is a multi-arc bildungsroman that blends gothic atmosphere with an unflinching portrait of a woman who refuses to surrender her self-respect for passion or security. It offers a narrative of endurance and autonomy wrapped in romance and mystery, carrying readers from the cruelty of childhood to a conclusion shaped by moral courage and hard-won joy.

If you were an agent and this landed on your desk...

What do you think? Does this sound like a story you'd want to read? Does it sound like the author has control of her material? What's working in this summary? Is there anything about it that makes you nervous?

Strengths: What comes across clearly here is that Jane Eyre is a powerful character on a quest for independence. The narrative promises to be well-grounded thematically.

Stories with strong female leads aren't new in our market, but this novel is set in the Victorian era of England, when women were preferably seen but not heard. In contrast to this norm, Jane seems unafraid to stand up for herself, which makes her even more intriguing as a protagonist.

Snags: Is the gothic element necessary? Will it serve the story or feel tacked on? That's really the only snag we can spot, and it's more of a question to keep in mind rather than a stumbling block. That said, it might also be problematic that the protagonist's love interest locks his mentally ill wife in the attic while attempting to lure Jane into polygamy without her knowledge.

Overall: A novel with a strong female lead is always a plus. A strong female lead in an environment where women were not welcomed to that role is even more intriguing. If Brontë can pull this off, it could be a big hit. Most agents would likely be excited to read the opening pages and see if she's got the chops to make this story work.

Part Three:
(Not Fake) First Pages

Your opening is really your best shot at winning over an agent or editor. It's called a hook for a reason. This is how you catch someone's attention: with a strong story written well. But the flip side: screw it up and there's no coming back from it. Does this sound like a lot of pressure for these poor pages to withstand? It is. You must get them right. Everything depends on it.

In this section, we step away from the (fake) query letters and synopses of our dead authors to the (not fake) opening pages of each of these classic novels. At this point, the exercise we're undertaking—the hypothetical assessment of these classic novels from a contemporary perspective— requires an extra-large grain of salt. Expectations of narrative structure haven't changed all that much over the years, but what has evolved considerably is POV, voice, writing style, and the modern demand for a hook (the quicker and sharper the better). We want to be clear—we think the novels we're critiquing are fantastic. But it's still worthwhile to consider how they could miss the mark if the authors were pitching them today, and then consider how these misfires might apply to our own work.

Keep your impressions of the query letters and synopses in mind. Do these writing samples surprise or delight you? Are they more (or less) than what you might have expected based on the rest of the submission? And if you discover that the writing sample is much better than you expected, what does this make you think about the importance of the query letter and/or synopsis?

Keep that agent's hat firmly on your head as you read through these pages. Imagine yourself at your desk, opening the fiftieth email of the day. Maybe today you've read six submissions about dog parks and six more about vampires. Maybe you just want to go home and put up your feet, have a glass of wine, and binge-watch the newest series. But this next submission could be *it*—the publishing world's next big thing. You could discover a fabulous new author. That's the hope that keeps you going every day: that one of these submissions will contain something brilliant.

Yes, agents are tired and overworked. Yes, they get thousands of submissions every year, and most of them are crap. But here's the thing: If you're good as an author, agents *want* to find you. They're looking for you. They don't just reject everyone out of hand. This is a business. They're in it to make money. They're looking for an idea that is marketable, something that will catch fire in some way. As an author, it's worth keeping that in mind. If your work is good, they'll want to read it.

All right, let's turn to the writing and see if these five authors can deliver. Let's see if they can make you miss your subway stop—which is the classic barometer for a submission so engaging it creates full immersion and makes a literary agent forget where they are.

Hook Assessment #1: Pride and Prejudice

It is a truth universally acknowledged, that a single man in possession of a good fortune, must be in want of a wife.

However little known the feelings or views of such a man may be on his first entering a neighbourhood, this truth is so well fixed in the minds of the surrounding families, that he is considered as the rightful property of some one or other of their daughters.

"My dear Mr. Bennet," said his lady to him one day, "have you heard that Netherfield Park is let at last?"

Mr. Bennet replied that he had not.

"But it is," returned she; "for Mrs. Long has just been here, and she told me all about it."

Mr. Bennet made no answer.

"Do not you want to know who has taken it?" cried his wife impatiently.

"*You* want to tell me, and I have no objection to hearing it."

This was invitation enough.

"Why, my dear, you must know, Mrs. Long says that Netherfield is taken by a young man of large fortune from the north of England; that he came down on Monday in a chaise and four to see the place, and was so much delighted with it that he agreed with Mr. Morris immediately; that he is to take possession before Michaelmas, and some of his servants are to be in the house by the end of next week."

"What is his name?"

"Bingley."

"Is he married or single?"

"Oh! Single, my dear, to be sure! A single man of large fortune; four or five thousand a year. What a fine thing for our girls!"

"How so? How can it affect them?"

"My dear Mr. Bennet," replied his wife, "how can you be so tiresome? You must know that I am thinking of his marrying one of them."

"Is that his design in settling here?"

"Design! Nonsense, how can you talk so! But it is very likely that he *may* fall in love with one of them, and therefore you must visit him as soon as he comes."

"I see no occasion for that. You and the girls may go, or you may send them by themselves, which perhaps will be still better, for as you are as handsome as any of them, Mr. Bingley might like you the best of the party."

"My dear, you flatter me. I certainly have had my share of beauty, but I do not pretend to be anything extraordinary now. When a woman has five grown-up daughters, she ought to give over thinking of her own beauty."

"In such cases, a woman has not often much beauty to think of."

"But, my dear, you must indeed go and see Mr. Bingley when he comes into the neighbourhood."

"It is more than I engage for, I assure you."

"But consider your daughters. Only think what an establishment it would be for one of them. Sir William and Lady Lucas are determined to go, merely on that account, for in general, you know, they visit no newcomers. Indeed you must go, for it will be impossible for us to visit him if you do not."

If you were an agent and this landed on your desk...

What would you do with this sample? How would you evaluate all that dialogue?

Strengths: There's plenty of white space on this page. Dialogue is a good tool for making a scene move, and this conversation moves well, with lots of back-and-forth between the two speakers. Austen has a great ear for conversation.

She sets up the situation quickly and gets the scene on its feet. We sense Mrs. Bennet's desire—five daughters, none married, and Mr. Hunk has just rolled into town, single and loaded. We also sense the irony that in a novel about marriage we meet a married couple that does nothing but bicker. We know from the pitch and synopsis that this story won't be about them, and yet this opening gives us a good sense of what's at stake. That makes it a pretty decent hook.

Snags: While Austen is mercifully brief with her context, the dialogue muscles in and takes over at the expense of almost everything else. She could easily have added some beats to this dialogue to round it out. Instead, the conversation takes place in a physical vacuum. Austen doesn't provide a single sensory detail or snippet of setting, which means the reader doesn't know where or how to visualize this scene. While the dialogue does reveal the characters of both Mr. and Mrs. Bennet and there is some tension in it—as well as humour—it also feels like it goes in circles and is perhaps longer than it needs to be.

Overall: We were quite surprised when we considered this opening sample against modern conventions, since we happen to know that the novel in question is so wonderful. If we had been the ones evaluating it based only on this page and we were in a foul mood, we might have rejected it. After all, the lack of sensory detail equates to a lack of immersive potential, and these days quick immersion is important. If we were feeling generous, we would keep reading with the hope that Austen's skill at writing dialogue would translate into other strengths in due course—but we'd be looking for an immersive scene to coalesce on page two. If that didn't happen, we'd probably give this one a miss.

Hook Assessment #2: Wuthering Heights

1801—I have just returned from a visit to my landlord—the solitary neighbour that I shall be troubled with. This is certainly a beautiful country! In all England, I do not believe that I could have fixed on a situation so completely removed from the stir of society. A perfect misanthropist's Heaven—and Mr. Heathcliff and I are such a suitable pair to divide the desolation between us. A capital fellow! He little imagined how my heart warmed towards him when I beheld his black eyes withdraw so suspiciously under their brows, as I rode up, and when his fingers sheltered themselves, with a jealous resolution, still further in his waistcoat, as I announced my name.

"Mr. Heathcliff?" I said.

A nod was the answer.

"Mr. Lockwood, your new tenant, sir. I do myself the honour of calling as soon as possible after my arrival, to express the hope that I have not inconvenienced you by my perseverance in soliciting the occupation of Thrushcross Grange: I heard yesterday you had had some thoughts—"

"Thrushcross Grange is my own, sir," he interrupted, wincing. "I should not allow any one to inconvenience me, if I could hinder it—walk in!"

The "walk in" was uttered with closed teeth, and expressed the sentiment, "Go to the Deuce!" even the gate over which he leant manifested no sympathising movement to the words; and I think that circumstance determined me to accept the invitation: I felt interested in a man who seemed more exaggeratedly reserved than myself.

When he saw my horse's breast fairly pushing the barrier, he did put out his hand to unchain it, and then sullenly preceded me up the causeway, calling, as we entered the court,— "Joseph, take Mr. Lockwood's horse; and bring up some wine."

"Here we have the whole establishment of domestics, I suppose," was the reflection suggested by this compound order. "No wonder the grass grows up between the flags, and cattle are the only hedge-cutters."

Joseph was an elderly, nay, an old man, very old, perhaps, though hale and sinewy.

"The Lord help us!" he soliloquised in an undertone of peevish displeasure, while relieving me of my horse: looking, meantime, in my face so sourly that I charitably conjectured he must have need of divine aid to digest his dinner, and his pious ejaculation had no reference to my unexpected advent.

Wuthering Heights is the name of Mr. Heathcliff's dwelling. "Wuthering" being a significant provincial adjective, descriptive of the atmospheric tumult to which its station is exposed in stormy weather. Pure, bracing ventilation they must have up there at all times, indeed: one may guess the power of the north wind, blowing over the edge, by the excessive slant of a few stunted firs at the end of the house; and by a range of gaunt thorns all stretching their limbs one way, as if craving alms of the sun. Happily, the architect had foresight to build it strong: the narrow windows are deeply set in the wall, and the corners defended with large jutting stones.

Before passing the threshold, I paused to admire a quantity of grotesque carving lavished over the front, and especially about the principal door; above which, among a wilderness of crumbling griffins and shameless little boys, I detected the date "1500," and the name "Hareton Earnshaw." I would have made a few comments, and requested a short history of the place from the surly owner; but his attitude at the door appeared to demand my speedy entrance, or complete departure, and I had no desire to aggravate his impatience previous to inspecting the penetralium.

If you were an agent and this landed on your desk...

Would this foray onto the moody English moors have made you miss your subway stop?

Strengths: Here's one reason why it might: tension. There's tension in nearly every aspect of this opening, from Heathcliff's grumpy behaviour to the stunted trees.

Here's another: voice. We gain immediate entry into the thoughts and emotions of the narrator, Mr. Lockwood, as he "tells" his story by way of a diary entry. While this strategy has the potential to backfire, Brontë makes it work by not treating it as a static device. We leap into scene and get snapshots right away of both Heathcliff and the landscape. These snapshots are important. Consider the visual specificity that's created here versus the "darkness" of bare dialogue in the opening to *Pride and Prejudice*. As readers, we depend on visualization to immerse ourselves in a fictional world. We're looking for guidance almost right away, and if you don't give it to us, we'll reach for another form of entertainment (probably our phone). We cannot visualize a scene that takes place in a vacuum.

If you're not familiar with Stephen King's iconic craft book, *On Writing*, go grab it and have a look at how he describes writing as a form of telepathy. That's the author's job in a nutshell: to transmit whatever is in your mind to the reader's mind, via the page. Brontë must have understood this intuitively because she uses sensory detail and description to anchor us right away in her fictional world. We see exactly what she sees, and it's so compelling we can't look away.

She also does a wonderful job of using POV to create intrigue. Heathcliff winces and looks suspiciously at Lockwood. Even though he rented Thrushcross Grange to Lockwood, he doesn't seem to want him there. Why? We don't know yet, but already we're curious to discover more. This first page is an object lesson in why a close POV is often more valuable to you than omniscience. We do not need to know what everyone in the room is thinking; in fact, it might be better if we don't.

We also get a sense that this author understands the dimensions of character. Heathcliff seems like a surly man, but he cares for the horse, and he seems inclined to at least attempt to be a decent host. If he's the antagonist, we can already see he won't be cardboard.

Snags: The only question we found ourselves asking is, why use Lockwood as a narrator? Why use this structure at all? He seems an odd choice for the POV, but we'd definitely want to read on to see what the author does with him.

Overall: This opening is a promising beginning that would likely make an agent ask for more.

Hook Assessment #3: The Scarlet Letter

THE CUSTOM-HOUSE

INTRODUCTORY TO "THE SCARLET LETTER"

It is a little remarkable, that—though disinclined to talk overmuch of myself and my affairs at the fireside, and to my personal friends—an autobiographical impulse should twice in my life have taken possession of me, in addressing the public. The first time was three or four years since, when I favored the reader—inexcusably, and for no earthly reason, that either the indulgent reader or the intrusive author could imagine—with a description of my way of life in the deep quietude of an Old Manse. And now—because, beyond my deserts, I was happy enough to find a listener or two on the former occasion—I again seize the public by the button, and talk of my three years' experience in a Custom-House. The example of the famous "P. P., Clerk of this Parish," was never more faithfully followed. The truth seems to be, however, that, when he casts his leaves forth upon the wind, the author addresses, not the many who will fling aside his volume, or never take it up, but the few who will understand him, better than most of his schoolmates or lifemates. Some authors, indeed, do far more than this, and indulge themselves in such confidential depths of revelation as could fittingly be addressed, only and exclusively, to the one heart and mind of perfect sympathy; as if the printed book, thrown at large on the wide world, were certain to find out the divided segment of the writer's own nature, and complete his circle of existence by bringing him into communion with it. It is scarcely decorous, however, to speak all, even where we speak impersonally. But, as thoughts are frozen and utterance benumbed, unless the speaker stand in some true relation with his audience, it may be pardonable to imagine that a friend, a kind and apprehensive, though not the closest friend, is listening to our talk; and then, a native reserve being thawed by this genial consciousness, we may prate of the circumstances that lie around us, and even of ourself, but still keep the inmost Me behind its veil. To this extent, and within these limits, an author, methinks, may be autobiographical, without violating either the reader's rights or his own.

It will be seen, likewise, that this Custom-House sketch has a certain propriety, of a kind always recognized in literature, as explaining how a large portion of the following pages came into my possession, and as offering proofs of the authenticity of a narrative therein contained. This, in fact,—a desire to put myself in my true position as editor, or very little more, of the most prolix among the tales that make up my volume,—this, and no other, is my true reason for assuming a personal relation with the public. In accomplishing the main purpose, it has appeared allowable, by a few extra touches, to give a faint representation of a mode of life not heretofore described, together with some of the characters that move in it, among whom the author happened to make one.

If you were an agent and this landed on your desk...

Well? Would you have kept reading? Or would you have thrown this page across the room?

Strengths: Are there any?

This is not an easy page to sink into. But let's set aside our fake-dead hypothetical for a moment. What Hawthorne is doing with this opening is establishing both the narrator and the genre. Historical fiction was just finding its feet in 1850, so with this Custom-House introduction, the author is giving us a frame of reference: here we have a "modern" narrator sharing a tale from an earlier time, both from the perspective of the documents he has unearthed and his own reflective perspective. In discussing the autobiographical nature of his narration, he creates a connection between himself and the protagonist, Hester Prynne. Like her, he feels alienated and misunderstood, so he offers up Hester's story to "the few who will understand him," as if, through her tale, he himself may be understood.

But here we are with our agent hats on. We don't have the privilege of Hawthorne's greater context, or of the entire introduction—because it's *long*. We have to admit, we're not finding much compulsion to turn the page and fear we might not be among those few who will understand him.

Snags: The whole thing is a snag. If we were agents, we would have sent a quick rejection. With vigour. This opening is, in a word, dull. Even though it's personalized with a first-person narrator, it is so unlike the opening of

Wuthering Heights the comparison is noteworthy. This opening is sunk by excessive and unnecessary wordiness. We barely made it to the end of the page. Why? No scene. Like Lockwood, this narrator is speaking, but he's telling rather than showing. You can get away with that for a little while if the voice is exceptional. But in this case, it isn't.

Publishing was certainly different when Hawthorne was writing, but now? If you can't grab an agent in that opening page, forget it. If your story "really gets going by page fifteen," then start it at page fifteen or else find some way to add more zip to the first fourteen pages.

Hawthorne doesn't help his case with that long opening paragraph. Visuals are important. When we see a dense opening like that, we immediately steel ourselves for something heavy. White space suggests movement. The eye can relax. Does this seem irrelevant? Test it out yourself by opening various books and seeing which are more hospitable to the eye based on the amount of white space. It makes a surprising difference.

Overall: Form rejection here. We can't see a single reason to read on based on this opening. If we were Hawthorne's editor, we'd advise him to ditch the intro and lead with chapter one—and definitely not quit his day job.

Hook Assessment #4: Anne of Green Gables

Mrs. Rachel Lynde lived just where the Avonlea main road dipped down into a little hollow, fringed with alders and ladies' eardrops and traversed by a brook that had its source away back in the woods of the old Cuthbert place; it was reputed to be an intricate, headlong brook in its earlier course through those woods, with dark secrets of pool and cascade; but by the time it reached Lynde's Hollow it was a quiet, well-conducted little stream, for not even a brook could run past Mrs. Rachel Lynde's door without due regard for decency and decorum; it probably was conscious that Mrs. Rachel was sitting at her window, keeping a sharp eye on everything that passed, from brooks and children up, and that if she noticed anything odd or out of place she would never rest until she had ferreted out the whys and wherefores thereof.

There are plenty of people, in Avonlea and out of it, who can attend closely to their neighbours' business by dint of neglecting their own; but Mrs. Rachel Lynde was one of those capable creatures who can manage their own concerns and those of other folks into the bargain. She was a notable housewife; her work was always done and well done; she "ran" the sewing circle, helped run the Sunday-school, and was the strongest prop of the Church Aid Society and Foreign Missions Auxiliary. Yet with all this Mrs. Rachel found abundant time to sit for hours at her kitchen window, knitting "cotton warp" quilts—she had knitted sixteen of them, as Avonlea housekeepers were wont to tell in awed voices—and keeping a sharp eye on the main road that crossed the hollow and wound up the steep red hill beyond. Since Avonlea occupied a little triangular peninsula jutting out into the Gulf of St. Lawrence, with water on two sides of it, anybody who went out of it or into it had to pass over that hill road and so run the unseen gauntlet of Mrs. Rachel's all-seeing eye.

She was sitting there one afternoon in early June. The sun was coming in at the window warm and bright; the orchard on the slope below the house was in a bridal flush of pinky-white bloom, hummed over by a myriad of bees. Thomas Lynde—a meek little man whom Avonlea people called

"Rachel Lynde's husband"—was sowing his late turnip seed on the hill field beyond the barn; and Matthew Cuthbert ought to have been sowing his on the big red brook field away over by Green Gables. Mrs. Rachel knew that he ought because she had heard him tell Peter Morrison the evening before in William J. Blair's store over at Carmody that he meant to sow his turnip seed the next afternoon. Peter had asked him, of course, for Matthew Cuthbert had never been known to volunteer information about anything in his whole life.

And yet here was Matthew Cuthbert, at half-past three on the afternoon of a busy day, placidly driving over the hollow and up the hill; moreover, he wore a white collar and his best suit of clothes, which was plain proof that he was going out of Avonlea; and he had the buggy and the sorrel mare, which betokened that he was going a considerable distance. Now, where was Matthew Cuthbert going, and why was he going there?

If you were an agent and this landed on your desk...

What stands out about this writing sample? If you recall, when we were talking about Montgomery's query letter, it seemed as though voice might be the make-or-break issue. Voice would reveal all: does this author have her "anecdotal" material under control, or will this be a nightmare?

Strengths: In our opinion, voice is what raises this sample to the top of the heap. It's brilliant. We meet Mrs. Rachel Lynde, the busybody of the town, who is described by the narrator with both humour and gentle sarcasm. Right away, we get a sense of this humour in the way the landscape is described—even the brooks and streams are conscious of Mrs. Lynde and know they'd better toe the line.

The opening begins with some summary writing, but Montgomery wastes no time getting her story off the ground. It shifts quickly into specifics: one afternoon in early June, the day something different happens. The day Matthew Cuthbert gets dressed up and sets off out of town to do something that Mrs. Rachel Lynde is not privy to.

She's dying to know where he's going. And with the sample ending there, we might be inclined to call this author on the phone and say, "We also need to know where he's going. Send more, ASAP."

What has Montgomery done here that's so effective?

- She has created intrigue.
- She has established a fantastic omniscient voice.
- She has not squandered that voice by spending too long in a character's head. The story moves almost immediately.
- She has set clear stakes for the protagonist: here is one of the many characters Anne will need to win over if she hopes to find her place in Avonlea.

Snags: There's a lot to be convinced by here. We can't imagine an agent not turning the page. But still, times have changed and so have market expectations. *Anne of Green Gables* is considered a middle-grade novel, especially since Anne Shirley is eleven at the beginning of the tale, though given the elevated language, some might say this would be more appropriately targeted to teens. An agent might wonder what the publisher's marketing team will make of this. They are pretty strict nowadays about a protagonist's age determining the audience (an eleven-year-old protagonist usually means a nine-year-old reader). Plus, most contemporary middle-grade novels will have simpler vocabulary and sentence structure, and they won't generally employ an omniscient narrator. Opening the story with an adult in focus is also unconventional.

Are any of these issues enough to sink the submission? We don't think so—not at this stage, at least. While market questions will need to be addressed eventually, Montgomery's first page reassures us we're in the hands of an expert storyteller.

Overall: Montgomery's query letter may have threatened to sink the project, but it has been more than salvaged by the writing sample, proving the point that the initial pitch might not be as important as you think. But the writing sample? It must shine. There's no *vice versa* about this situation. If your query letter is great but the sample stinks, you've lost your chance.

Hook Assessment #5: Jane Eyre

There was no possibility of taking a walk that day. We had been wandering, indeed, in the leafless shrubbery an hour in the morning; but since dinner (Mrs. Reed, when there was no company, dined early) the cold winter wind had brought with it clouds so sombre, and a rain so penetrating, that further outdoor exercise was now out of the question.

I was glad of it: I never liked long walks, especially on chilly afternoons: dreadful to me was the coming home in the raw twilight, with nipped fingers and toes, and a heart saddened by the chidings of Bessie, the nurse, and humbled by the consciousness of my physical inferiority to Eliza, John, and Georgiana Reed.

The said Eliza, John, and Georgiana were now clustered round their mama in the drawing-room: she lay reclined on a sofa by the fireside, and with her darlings about her (for the time neither quarrelling nor crying) looked perfectly happy. Me, she had dispensed from joining the group; saying, "She regretted to be under the necessity of keeping me at a distance; but that until she heard from Bessie, and could discover by her own observation that I was endeavouring in good earnest to acquire a more sociable and childlike disposition, a more attractive and sprightly manner—something lighter, franker, more natural, as it were—she really must exclude me from privileges intended only for contented, happy, little children."

"What does Bessie say I have done?" I asked.

"Jane, I don't like cavillers or questioners; besides, there is something truly forbidding in a child taking up her elders in that manner. Be seated somewhere; and until you can speak pleasantly, remain silent."

A breakfast-room adjoined the drawing-room, I slipped in there. It contained a bookcase: I soon possessed myself of a volume, taking care that it should be one stored with pictures. I mounted into the window-seat: gathering up my feet, I sat cross-legged, like a Turk; and, having drawn the red moreen curtain nearly close, I was shrined in double retirement.

Folds of scarlet drapery shut in my view to the right hand; to the left were the clear panes of glass, protecting, but not separating me from the drear November day. At intervals, while turning over the leaves of my book, I studied the aspect of that winter afternoon. Afar, it offered a pale blank of mist and cloud; near, a scene of wet lawn and storm-beat shrub, with ceaseless rain sweeping away wildly before a long and lamentable blast.

I returned to my book—Bewick's *History of British Birds*: the letterpress thereof I cared little for, generally speaking; and yet there were certain introductory pages that, child as I was, I could not pass quite as a blank. They were those which treat of the haunts of sea-fowl; of "the solitary rocks and promontories" by them only inhabited; of the coast of Norway, studded with isles from its southern extremity, the Lindeness, or Naze, to the North Cape—

"Where the Northern Ocean, in vast whirls,
Boils round the naked, melancholy isles
Of farthest Thule; and the Atlantic surge
Pours in among the stormy Hebrides."

If you were an agent and this landed on your desk...

What would you think? Would you ask to see the first three chapters? The whole novel? What jumps out at you as fabulous or intriguing? Is there anything you think might need work?

Strengths: One thing this opening has going for it is conflict. We don't know much yet about Jane's living situation, but we can tell her stasis is not a happy one. This is an important point. Stasis involves establishing the protagonist's norm before it gets knocked sideways. But "the norm" doesn't mean same old, same old. Far from it! There should always be tension simmering somewhere in those opening pages, and here we have it in abundance. Jane evaluates herself beside the three children she lives with and finds herself wanting. She's an outsider; this is not her family, and from what we see in this opening, the mother makes her irritation very evident. Even the weather is moody.

Another thing that strikes us right away is that Jane is smart. We know she's fond of reading and is likely an introvert, since she's quite happy to tuck herself away in the window seat with a book.

Brontë adds plenty of sensory detail to ground us in the physical scene. This is also important. She doesn't overwhelm the reader with detail, but she gives us enough that we can visualize the action and locale. Remember, if you don't supply your reader with a few key details, you will fail to establish reader immersion, which will likely net you a rejection letter.

Brontë also adds dialogue, and it is conversation with a purpose. It reveals both Jane's character (she does not accept things at face value) and Mrs. Reed's (she is unpleasant and resents Jane's very presence).

Snags: The only thing we would have liked to know sooner is Jane's age. It's hard to imagine her without knowing how old she is. But that's a small thing and easily fixed. We could have also perhaps done with less of Bewick's *History of British Birds*. How much of that does the reader really need? Once upon a time, novels could ease readers in slowly. Nowadays, readers expect an author to get the show on the road quickly, especially when it comes to the opening hook.

Overall: All the pluses here add up to potential: this is a pot that's already set to boil over at any moment. The voice is strong. We sense a plucky character in Jane, which makes her someone we'd like to know more about. The snags are slight and wouldn't stop us from asking to see the rest of the manuscript.

Welcome to Query Quest. You've played the part of literary agent evaluating five great classic novels in terms of their marketability. Now it's time to take what you've learned, put on your author hat, and examine this process from the point of view of your own masterpiece-in-progress.

In this section, we'll take a closer look at five key elements of the querying process:

- The query letter
- The synopsis
- The writing sample
- The importance of getting feedback
- The querying process itself

This is the how-to (and sometimes how-not-to) section of the book. We have interviewed more than a hundred agents, judged thousands of query letters, synopses, and first pages in Darling Axe contests, and edited scores of manuscripts (including our own). From there, we have boiled down the process to some basic guidelines to follow when it comes to sending out your work and hopefully winning the attention of an agent.

Keep in mind not every agent will want exactly the same things, so it's vital that you tailor your submissions to the specific guidelines of each. "Follow instructions" might sound like such a simple rule that it's not worth mentioning, but a surprising number of people do not follow agents' instructions, and, as a result, their submission goes straight to the bin.

Don't spoil your chances right out of the gate. Read each agent's guidelines carefully and only send what they ask for. Your submission should stand out because of the writing—not because you included a mood board or sent in a 5,000-word synopsis because your novel is so complex that the 500 words they asked for couldn't possibly do it justice.

Above all, don't rush. You'll hear us say this over and over. That's how important it is. Even if you've met an agent at a conference who asked for your first three chapters, but then some nasty editor (probably one of us) informed you that those chapters weren't ready—still, don't rush. The agent will wait. They'd rather read a stellar submission that arrives two months late than a mediocre one that they'll dismiss after the first page.

You don't get a second chance to make a good first impression with an agent. Once they've read and dismissed your submission, you can cross them off the list. Unless they've specifically asked you to revise and resubmit, they don't want to hear from you again on the same novel.

Don't squander that chance! Take your time and do it right.

How to Write a Query Letter

Contrary to what you might think, it is not a query letter's job to sell your manuscript; the manuscript itself will do that heavy lifting (or not). What your query letter needs to do is spark interest. Yes, it's critical to follow the submission guidelines and write a compelling pitch, but everything else is secondary.

Finding the right literary agent for your manuscript requires doing a bit of homework. Once you've found someone whose interests align with yours, convincing them that your project is polished and marketable is another battle altogether. If you want to work with the agent of your dreams, you must put in the time, effort, and research to make your dream a reality.

The most important consideration is that your manuscript fits their criteria—that it's a genre they represent. Next, consider their client list. Are they promoting books that feel like a good match with your own work? Finally, narrow in on your ideal candidates based on whether you'd like to work with them. Can you imagine yourself in a long-term business relationship with this agent? This final step may take some digging: their agent profile is the obvious starting point, but you might also uncover interesting tidbits in interviews, on personal blogs, and on social media. The Book Broker series on the Darling Axe blog includes over a hundred interviews with top literary agents and is worth checking out.

You might be tempted to skip that last step because you figure you'll be happy with any agent who will take you. Don't. Not all agents are created equal, and not all will be the right fit for you, your personality, your work, your goals. This really is a partnership, and both partners need to be enthusiastic about the match.

Ten Tips for a Strong Query Letter

1. A query letter shouldn't exceed one page. This is a teaser for your project, so short and sweet is best. That being said, since a query letter often takes the form of an email these days, aim for fewer than 500 words. Some agents say they prefer queries to be 250-350 words.

2. As mentioned before (though it bears repeating), follow submission guidelines. They differ from one agent to the next. Don't get cute about it. Only give them what they ask for.

3. The most important part of your query letter is the pitch (we'll do a deep dive into pitches in the next chapter), so make sure yours is as sharp as it can be.

4. If you're going to include comparable titles, don't compare yourself to the greats. Choose two or three recent mid-list titles instead. By recent, we mean published in the last two or three years. That's because comp titles aren't meant to give a plot comparison so much as a demonstration that your book has a place in the current market.

5. Make sure the query letter is well written—no grammatical or spelling errors, no unnecessary hype. Don't tell the agent how much they're going to love your hard-hitting or hilarious manuscript. Let them come to those conclusions on their own.

6. Don't submit to more than one agent in the same agency. They will refer you internally if they think another agent on their team is a better fit.

7. Don't send the exact same query to every agent. Even a small amount of personalization can go a long way.

8. Swap query-letter critiques with other writers in online forums. Anonymous strangers can be pretty brutal with their feedback, but if you have the backbone for it, workshopping your query online can be helpful. You might also consider a (gentler and often more effective) query critique service.

9. Don't send the first query letter you write to hundreds of agents. Send it to five, wait a couple weeks, then rewrite your query (and your synopsis, and quite possibly also your opening pages) and try five more. Rejections and silence are good indications that your query or opening pages need more work.

10. Most importantly, make sure your manuscript is in the best shape it can be. Arrange feedback swaps with other writers, not friends and family. You should go through a few rounds of development and revision (at a minimum) before you start querying.

These are tips, not rules. If you've done much research into the art of the query letter, you may have noticed plenty of (often conflicting) advice about paragraph order, personalization, comp titles, etc. However, if you look at some successful query samples (for example, from Eric Smith's blog, *Perfect Pitch*), you'll find many of them break a rule or two. Experiment with what works best for your specific project.

Ideally, your query letter will spark hope in the agent that they've found the next great novel. Agents receive, on average, more than a thousand queries per year and offer representation to only a handful. Yours must stand out—and not with sparkles and colourful font. The writing, the concept—these are what make an excellent query.

To Personalize or Not to Personalize…?

The pitch is paramount in a query letter, but strategic personalization also helps. While it won't make or break a submission, it shows agents that you're not just spamming anyone and everyone. A personalized letter feels more professional and shows you're taking a targeted approach.

In our Book Broker agent interview series, Meg Davis (Ki Agency) says she values personalization for its signal of intent: "Personalisation is a good sign the author is taking themselves seriously and asking me to as well." It seems more like you're looking for connection. A relationship—which is ideally what the author/agent arrangement will look like. However, not all agents need personalization. As Mary C. Moore (Aevitas Creative Management) puts it, "Honestly, if the query spells my name right and falls within the category I represent, that's enough personalization for me."

Bottom line: the pitch is the most critical part of your query letter, but personalizing it will make you look professional, and that might affect how an agent views your submission.

When Word Count Is a Red Flag

Bigger is not always better. Word count can be an important red flag in terms of a manuscript's readiness for publication. When you stray too far from genre norms, an agent will start asking questions about structure, editing, and how the heck to market a 160,000-word novel about miniature dogs. As agent Katelyn Uplinger says, "A word count that is far over or under the genre standard usually means underdeveloped plots and characters or poor pacing and a rambling plot."

An excessively long manuscript might suggest that the author doesn't know how to edit their own work. It might seem like an accomplishment to have written a doorstopper, but the reality is that the novel is probably suffering from bloat, and more pages translate into higher printing costs. That hefty 160k-word novel will also require more extensive editing. Twice as much, in fact, as two 80k-word novels. On top of that, readers are less likely to buy a longer book from an author they've never heard of.

Yes, Stephen King and George R.R. Martin have written gigantic tomes in their time, but they've got the sales power behind them to get away with it.

That doesn't mean the answer is to go small. If your manuscript is significantly under the expected word count, there's a chance it will lack depth. An agent will be on the lookout for thin characters and a plot that's too straightforward (and therefore too predictable). As Sharon Pelletier emphasizes, deviations from word count norms can indicate that the author hasn't "rigorously and thoughtfully edited their work."

Ultimately, this is a debut issue. If you've proven yourself with prior publications, you can get away with breaking more rules than a fledgling novelist trying to crack the market for the first time.

Don't Stress Over Comp Titles

In the labyrinth of the querying world, it's easy to hang all your hopes and fears on comparable titles and the market paragraph of your query letter. However, whether an agent asks to read your full manuscript will ultimately be decided by the opening pages. Comp titles are the cherry on the cake, not the cake itself.

At their worst, your comp titles might be either overly ambitious or outdated. We all want to be the next Tolkien or Hemingway, but it's the sort of thing you shouldn't say out loud—or in a query letter. It sounds presumptuous, it's almost certainly not true, and it indicates that you don't understand the current market. Similarly, using out-of-date books or referencing only films or shows might suggest you're not actively engaging with the contemporary literary scene. Either that or you haven't read a novel since high school.

Sure, it helps to know which books your potential audience is currently reading, but don't place too much importance on the various query-letter components. If your query letter is adequate, most agents will take a closer look. If all you're receiving are form rejections and radio silence, go back to your opening pages. Sorry to say it, because it's harder to fix than a lazy comp or a lack of personalization, but the most likely source of the problem is the writing itself.

The Power of a Pitch

Your pitch is the most important part of your query letter. Literary agents are on the hunt for great stories, after all. Publishing cred, well-researched comp titles, and a bit of personalization will certainly help, but your pitch is the real currency. As it should be. This is the essence of your story. It's why you're so excited about it, so you'll want to convey that excitement in a way that makes it contagious.

Concept and Craft

A pitch should convey two basic things: you know how to write, and you've got one hell of an idea. As literary agent Sarah Davies puts it, "I'm always looking for the two *C* words—concept and craft." Not confusion. Not chaos.

A pitch is a teaser, an amuse-bouche for the novel. It should be short and to the point. It does not have to reveal the whole story, nor should it: that's what a synopsis is for. Think "back cover of a novel," and that gives you a good idea of what a pitch should look like. A back-cover blurb is usually the first thing a reader turns to when they're deciding whether to buy a book. That's what your pitch has to do for an agent: *Do I want to read this whole manuscript on my own precious time, for free?* Because, remember, they don't get paid until they sign you with a publisher.

Demonstrating Craft Savvy

A significant part of a novel's art lies in its structure. Immersive details and scene-based writing will draw readers into your story world, but it's the power of narrative structure that keeps them turning pages.

But plot and structure are only one part of the equation. There are also the characters.

If your reader falls in love with your protagonist, it will keep them connected, invested, and eager to know what happens next, and characterization plays an important structural role. This is because characterization is best demonstrated through an arc: the protagonist embarks on a journey towards a goal, struggles, learns, and in the end is transformed in some way. It's all connected.

Literary agent Hannah Sheppard has developed an excellent pitch test or logline formula:

> *When A (inciting incident) happens, B (character) must do C (action) otherwise/before D (catastrophe).*

This is what an agent or publisher wants to see in your pitch—the essentials of the story. Sheppard's pitch test is also a great tool for making sure the structure of your novel is sound.

(Keep in mind that a story with multiple POV characters and/or plotlines may need to use the logline formula multiple times.)

Some Logline Examples

The Lord of the Rings: When a young hobbit is gifted a dangerous magical ring, he must leave behind all comfort and safety on a journey to stop evil from taking over the world.

The Great Gatsby: When a young man discovers that the love of his life has married someone else (who happens to be wealthy), he vows to get rich in order to win her back, else his life will be meaningless.

Moby-Dick: After losing his leg to a giant white whale, a sea captain's thirst for revenge threatens to consume him unless he can conquer his obsession.

The Shining: When a writer becomes the winter caretaker of a hotel, he must confront his personal demons or risk going mad and endangering his family.

The Hunger Games: When a teenager steps up to take her sister's place in the Hunger Games, she must battle an oppressive regime or face certain death.

Let's Get Practical: Putting the Pitch Test into Practice

Try boiling your novel down to one sentence. Hard? Yes. But it's doable.

Aim for five to ten different one-line pitches and focus on uncovering your novel's trajectory: what question does the story ask at the beginning that is answered by the end?

Once you're happy with your one-sentence pitch, expand it into two and then three sentences. That should give you a pretty solid plot-summary paragraph for your query letter that conveys character, craft, and concept.

A Fresh Concept

The average agent will easily review a thousand queries every year, and some as many as five thousand. It's not enough for your story to be "interesting" or even for it to have good bones. With that many queries in the mix, yours needs to stand out.

Enter the fresh concept, a key component of the query-letter pitch.

A fresh concept can be a shiny new idea or a creative take on something that's been done before. Either way, a fresh story makes an agent stop and think, *Now there's something I've never seen.* While it's important to highlight what's unique about your plot and characters, this isn't something you can fudge. Either it's new or it isn't. That's the stark reality. A story concept is fresh when it's legitimately a neat idea—a genesis or revival—and not simply because you've been creative with the wording of your pitch.

Part of hitting on a fresh concept is also luck, since you likely won't have access to all the ideas that are currently landing on agents' desks (or will be by next week). But beware the bandwagon effect. Both popular fiction and world events can inspire fads in creativity. A vampire novel will become a bestseller, and six months later agents' inboxes are filled with bloodsucking plotlines. Or you start spotting drones with some regularity at parks and festivals, and suddenly agents are inundated with science fiction thrillers based around drone warfare (those are both real examples, by the way).

Misfiring Pitches

We work with many clients on their query letters. Plus, we have the advice of many amazing agents who have taken the time to share their thoughts in our interviews. Here are some of the most common reasons for a pitch to fall flat:

- A focus on context (world-building, backstory) more than on the actual story
- A protagonist who doesn't have a specific goal
- A lack of clear stakes
- A general lack of clarity

Don't Query Too Soon

It's not easy to summarize an entire novel in one or two short paragraphs, but this is especially true of manuscripts with meandering and convoluted plotlines. If your narrative structure is watertight, your story will be easier to describe. If you're struggling to express the events of your novel with the above pitch test, then your narrative structure might still need an overhaul.

"But that means I have to rewrite it. It's already finished."

This is a reaction we've heard many times. But the reality is, you probably do have to rewrite it. Welcome to novel writing.

Most writers query long before they're actually ready. In other words, their manuscript is still in an early draft stage, or the writer has yet to fully wrap their head around narrative structure. To convince an agent to stand by your side and represent your work, your manuscript should be as close to perfection as you can get it. That means revision, workshopping with critique partners, more revision, maybe a bit more workshopping, and then a bit more revision.

The learning curve is steep and takes way longer than most writers want or expect. Many writers we work with are in a rush to be published. But the truth is, learning to write well is no different than learning to play the violin well. There's no substitute for time spent practising, and if you haven't done the work, it shows.

In the end, it's all a learning process: the writing, the revision, and the rejection too. With each "no" you're forced back to the drawing board to consider once again how you can tighten, tune, and transform your work.

A Query Letter in Building Blocks

Try drafting your own query letter using the following template:

Dear Agent (with their name spelled correctly).

First Paragraph: Include a brief personalization of why you think this person is the right one for your work. Add a basic introduction of the work that includes the title, the word count, and the genre.

Second Paragraph: Include the pitch, a brief (100-200 word) description of the book. Think jacket copy rather than a laundry list of what happens in the novel, which means focusing only on the main storyline and characters, their goals, the obstacles they face, and perhaps the theme.

Third Paragraph: Include two or three recent comp titles that might appeal to readers of your novel and explain why they're appropriate for your project.

Fourth Paragraph: Include your bio, which might consist of previous publications and awards, your writing education (including workshops and conferences you've been to), and any relevant experience or perspective you bring to this work.

Thank the agent for their time.

Include ONLY the secondary items (a synopsis and/or a certain number of opening pages) that have been requested in the submission guidelines.

Proofread, proofread, proofread.

Send.

Keep writing.

The Dreaded Synopsis

Many authors hate writing synopses... because they're hard. Sometimes that's because you're too close to your material to have that essential clarity for seeing the bigger picture. But usually, the issue is much simpler and more troublesome. The reason synopses are hard to write is because, more than any other tool available, they show you what's wrong with the novel you've labored over for months, if not years.

The synopsis is the equivalent of a house inspector—that person who walks around with a clipboard and goes through the home you thought you were ready to sell, pointing out all the structural issues you either didn't know about or pretended weren't a problem: roof damage, termites, a saggy bearing wall, you name it. You can do all the fancy writing in the world, but if there's something fundamentally wrong with your novel, it will come out in the synopsis.

That's why authors hate them—and why most agents ask for one.

The Moment of Truth

Reading a synopsis is the quickest way to find out if an author knows what they're doing when it comes to things like structure, causality, story arc, and characterization—you know, those critical developmental issues you hoped wouldn't matter.

Guess what? They do.

If your plot isn't constructed as a chain of causality, it will show up in the synopsis as a series of "and then this happened" events. If your protagonist doesn't have a clear, specific, and relatable goal that they're actively pursuing throughout the story, if there are no stakes, a weak antagonist, a plot that's bursting with too much superficial business and no depth—yup, the synopsis will reveal all of that.

If you, the author, are willing to see it, the synopsis can be that heart-sinking moment of truth where you can no longer deny that this house is not ready to sell, not by a long shot. It needs help. It might even need to be razed to the ground and built from scratch.

Too extreme, you say? Well, most published authors we know (ourselves included) have had to do it on numerous occasions. John Green does it with every one of his first drafts—throws out ninety percent, right down to the foundation, and starts over.

What do most new authors do? Close their eyes and send out the query as is, along with that stinky synopsis, hoping agents won't notice.

They'll notice.

If you wonder why your novel is getting rejected time and again, the synopsis may hold a clue. Even if the premise is great—which it may well be—if you can't execute it because of developmental issues, forget it. No one will ask to read it.

This is harsh. It's not what writers want to hear. But it's the truth.

How to Write a Synopsis

What is a synopsis, anyway?

A synopsis is a clear and direct summary of your manuscript that should highlight your engaging protagonist, their emotional arc, the originality of your vision, and the logic of your plot.

Notice that we mention plot last. While a plot summary is an important aspect of a synopsis—agents and publishers want to verify that your story has internal logic—the plot is only the framework. The true essence that keeps readers turning pages is everything in concert: emotional appeal, character motivation, the protagonist's relentless struggle towards a goal, and stakes. If your synopsis reads like Arnold Toynbee's definition of history ("one damned thing after another"), then you will have missed the mark.

Here are some guidelines to consider:

Particulars

- Stick to third person, present tense
- Use a standard font
- Highlight the first mention of character names in bold or CAPS

These are just guidelines. Check your would-be agent's submission requirements to be sure. Maybe they will only read synopses written in Comic Sans. Unlikely, but you never know.

Length

Opinions vary on the ideal length of a synopsis. Again, always check submission requirements. Some agents don't even want to see a synopsis. Others might ask for one as short as 250 words or as long as 2000. It's a good practice to have synopses of various lengths prepared in advance, just in case. If an agent asks for a synopsis but doesn't specify length, opt for shorter—about 500 words. Overall, however, the most common expectation seems to be a synopsis of no more than 1000 words.

Structure

Because you want to demonstrate to agents that you have a good grasp of narrative structure, aim to include those key turning points: inciting incident (and associated goal), rising action (obstacles that stand in the protagonist's way), and climax (outcome, whether success or failure). And don't forget the stakes: What does failure mean for your protagonist? Why should the reader care?

Reveal the plot through your characters, their motivations, their choices, the obstacles they encounter, and how their struggle affects them.

Some people recommend writing one or two sentences to summarize each chapter or scene, then hacking and slashing until everything's in place. However, what you might end up with is a dry plot summary or a synopsis that doesn't balance the most critical aspects of your storytelling. Try this approach if you like, but make sure you also represent the underlying narrative structure.

Additional Suggestions

- Only use dialogue if it's short and relevant
- Polish your synopsis—it represents both your writing AND storytelling ability
- Aim to be economical with your language rather than poetic
- Don't mention too many characters—only two or three if possible
- Don't cram in every subplot and side quest
- Minimize world-building terms and jargon
- Remember: characters carry the plot—focus on their motivations, decisions, emotions

We said not to stress over comp titles, that they aren't make-or-break, but a synopsis is a different story. It's worth taking the time to get it right and getting feedback on it before you send it out.

Let's Get Practical: A Synopsis in Building Blocks

Yes, we know: you'd rather not practice something this heinous, but we promise it's worth it. This activity will help you draft a compelling synopsis, which also means you'll get an opportunity to consider your story structure.

1) Identify the following structural elements in your story

Narrative motivation: What overarching desire is driving your protagonist to make choices and take risks? What underlying need, in opposition to this desire, is adding to their internal conflict?

Trajectory: Does the beginning of the story ask a question that is answered by the end? Hint: your protagonist's goal is the question, and the answer is whether they succeed or fail.

Stasis: This is the setting and/or circumstance that your protagonist finds themself in before the story truly gets started. It is what they will leave behind—perhaps what they need to overcome or what they stand to lose. And it's usually where the reader first discovers the protagonist's underlying motivation (which will crystallize into a narrative goal with the inciting incident). It's possible for the stasis to come before the story actually starts. It could be childhood, a relationship, a job, a place, or even an idea—whatever will change as the protagonist sets out in search of a new life, relationship, job, etc.

In a synopsis, your description of stasis and setting should be short and sweet. One sentence will be plenty for most stories, though works of speculative fiction may need a few more to establish key world-building details or histories. Beware in spec fiction of getting carried away here. Simplicity is key. If you overwhelm an agent with too much terminology or world-building, their eyes will glaze over, and the rest of the synopsis will be a blur. That said, if you need a flowchart to explain your world or magic system, the synopsis might not be the problem.

Inciting incident and point of no return: In nearly every story ever told, there is an inciting incident that marks the beginning of the protagonist's move away from stasis. Think: the first glimpse of a would-be lover, a phone call in the night, the death of a loved one. The antagonist, or a hint of the antagonist, often appears here as well. What normal aspect of the protagonist's life is disrupted at the start of your story? What sets the story in motion? Keep in mind that the inciting incident should line up with the climax like an arrow shot to a target. Whatever you set up at the beginning must match the outcome.

A point of no return usually follows the inciting incident—when the protagonist makes a choice that sets them on their path. Once this choice is made, it should be difficult or impossible to take it back (maybe not logistically, but emotionally and/or psychologically). The point of no return might immediately follow the inciting incident, or it might come later, as choices and conflicts accumulate. What critical choice does your protagonist make early on that locks them into a chain of consequence?

Rising action: This is the meat of the first and second act, everything that leads to the main crisis of the story. Reveal the plot through your characters, their motivations, their choices, the obstacles they encounter, and how their struggle affects them. Your protagonist AND antagonist are developed through rising action.

In both your synopsis and story, the characters should be driving the plot, not the other way around. Make sure they have agency—that their decisions and mistakes are what move things forward and build momentum—or else they'll seem more like puppets than people.

All is lost: This is the crisis that leads to the climax. Your protagonist has reached the narrative rock bottom: his love interest has left him; she's been fired from her job; they've lost the magical artifact they sought to protect. The antagonist is poised to win. Is there a dark moment leading up to the climax in which your protagonist hits bottom or it seems as if what they seek is beyond their reach?

False victory: If you're writing a tragedy, you will have a false victory instead of an all-is-lost moment. Your protagonist is poised to win; everything is looking up. But this is merely false hope, because the climax is where your protagonist will crash and burn, learning too late the errors of their ways.

The helping hand: Who or what helps the protagonist in their bleakest hour? If you use this structural element, be careful that this person doesn't end up solving the protagonist's problem for them. The protagonist should be doing all the heavy lifting. Often this involves a helpful nudge that enables the protagonist's epiphany and/or transformation.

Climax and resolution: Your story's climax is the scene in which the protagonist either achieves or fails to achieve their goal—whether they win back a lover, orchestrate an enemy's downfall, or are punished for their fatal flaw. The final lead-up to the climax might also include a hint about the closing emotional turns and relationship arcs that have underpinned the protagonist's motivations. What has your protagonist learned over the course of the novel that equips them to take on their final challenge? Do they achieve the goal that was forecast in the beginning? Or do they fail while learning something important in the process?

Avoid the temptation in a synopsis to leave an agent with a dramatic cliff-hanger. Agents and publishers want to know how your story ends so they can assess whether your ending makes logical sense. You don't have to go deep into the resolution, but you do want to show how the main conflict is resolved, and perhaps a hint about the closing emotional vibe.

If you can't identify some of the above elements, consider whether the story truly demands that they be omitted. If you've only left these things out because "that's the way the story ended up," then you likely have another draft ahead of you. Only the most experimental fiction subverts these structures, and it does so intentionally (and usually with a lot of experience).

2) Summarize your novel in five sentences

Sentence 1: the disruption of normal life (the inciting incident)

Sentences 2-4: the rising action of the second act (movement towards a goal and obstacles encountered along the way)

Sentence 5: the climax and resolution

3) Expand these five sentences into five short paragraphs

Aim for 100 words per paragraph for an approximate total of 500 words.

4) Set this aside, no peeking, and freewrite a 1000-word synopsis

You can be creative here, but also try to draw on what you've hammered out in the earlier stages. Aim for drama, character, structure, and stakes.

5) Compare your two synopses (500 and 1000)

Once you have two synopses, compare them, take what you like best from each, and draft a final 500-word synthesis of the two.

Keep in mind that this is A LOT to cram into a small space, so it's fine to omit some plot events and even subplots. Only the most essential characters need to make an appearance. A synopsis can be particularly challenging if your manuscript is a multi-POV because each focal character will ideally have their own goal, obstacles, and arc. You'll want to do the story justice, which means shining a light on the strongest threads. That could involve choosing which of your focal characters can be invited to the party and which need to stay home.

By this point, you should have a good idea of what should be included. By combining the more rigid plot summary with the freewritten synopsis, you will strike a nice balance of structure and voice.

Above all, take your time. Writing a synopsis is a daunting process for everyone, and unlike the query letter, structural snags actually can spoil your chances of landing an agent or a publishing deal.

Who's on Mic?
The Importance of Voice

It's time to shift away from query letters and synopses to the all-important writing sample. Literary agents frequently mention the critical role of voice in the manuscripts they evaluate. A compelling voice can often override other manuscript weaknesses because the latter are easier to fix. But if the voice isn't there, nothing else will save the novel.

In our Book Broker interviews, Ella Marie Shupe (Belcastro Agency) said, "A terrific voice and clever premise always capture my attention."

Andy Ross (Andy Ross Literary) describes voice as something "easy to see, usually in the first paragraph."

And agents like Karly Caserza (Fuse Literary) look for a voice that "establishes a strong presence right away," emphasizing the need for characters to project their essence clearly and compellingly from the first word.

You've probably met more than one sarcastic YA protagonist, so you'll already know that voice is more than a series of verbal tics or a particular tone. It's a character's unique way of being in the world. It's the lens through which your narrator views absolutely everything. Is it too much to call it the story's soul? No, we are unapologetically going out on that limb. Voice imbues your prose with immediacy, individuality, and authenticity.

What you're doing with voice is demonstrating personality. Voice creates connection—or not—between the reader and the story. Hard to pin down: yes. But like a ripe avocado, you know it when it's in your hands. Its presence is undeniable, and it often becomes the deciding factor in whether your manuscript engages or alienates readers from the very first paragraph.

Components of Voice

The voice in a manuscript is shaped by several components:

Diction: This means choosing words that are true to the character's background, education, and personality, so that you reflect their unique way of speaking and thinking. If a character grew up on the streets and just got out of prison, they probably won't sound like an Oxford professor (however, anything can work in the right hands).

Syntax: The way you arrange words and phrases into sentences can reveal a character's pace of thought, emotional state, and level of sophistication.

Character Perspective: Who a character is will dictate how they perceive their surroundings. What does your character notice? What do they ignore? When they walk into the room, do they fixate on the stained carpet? Are they evaluating square footage? Looking for secondary exits? Assessing the décor? Their background and interests should come through in the metaphors they use to describe and understand the world around them.

Narrative Distance: How close do you want the reader to feel to the character's thoughts and emotions? Fly on the wall, or intimately connected to every insight they have?

Common Pitfalls in Developing Voice

If you've struggled to nail the voice of your protagonist, it won't be news to you that there are pitfalls to avoid when crafting a strong voice:

Over-stylization: In other words, you're trying too hard. When you force uniqueness, it can make the voice feel contrived. Instead of drawing readers closer to the narrative, you'll push them away.

Inconsistency: Usually this happens if you don't know your characters all that well and *forget* what you've decided they sound like. These kinds of fluctuations in voice will confuse readers and disrupt the flow of the story. It's hard to connect with someone whose personality can't be pinned down.

Lack of Depth: This is another result of not knowing your characters well. The voice will feel flat and unconvincing because we're only getting the Facebook version of this person. In other words, superficial.

Unclear Character Motivations: The result of... you guessed it: not knowing your characters well enough. Their decisions should drive the story while also demonstrating who they are and what matters most to them. If you don't know who they are, you'll simply force them into a mechanical plot. But plot should be driven by characterization. What a character wants should shape their behavior. So if you're making these decisions based on what you think should happen rather than who they are, the story will feel motivationally contrived.

In Conclusion

If you hear someone say, "I just read this great book," chances are it's the voice they're responding to. Voice makes a novel resonate; it's what connects us to the story, making us cry or laugh, giving us things to think about long after we've closed the book. It elevates a story into an experience.

That's what we're doing in a novel, after all: we're creating an experience, inviting the reader to live through something and in something they've never encountered before. And when that's done well, it's unforgettable.

Setup Is Not Stasis: A First-Chapter Crime

Whether you're submitting a manuscript sample to a literary agent or a publisher, the strength of your first sentence, first page, and first chapter is vital. At this early stage, your most important job is to convince readers that it's worth their time to keep reading. You're opening a door for them, beckoning them into your story world; you want them to decide to stay.

Story Versus Context

We launched our Book Broker agent interview series back in 2018. To date, we've heard from over a hundred agents. What they have to say about chapter-one misfires aligns with what we frequently see in developmental edits and the hundreds of contest entries we screen each year.

> *I often see writers clearing their throats—writing out information about a character's background or past or over-explaining their situation instead of trusting their reader to piece things together for themselves.*
> —Tim Wojcik, LGR Literary Agency

When a first chapter isn't working, there is one resoundingly common issue: the author is showcasing *context* rather than *story*. In other words, they are telling rather than showing—presenting information rather than creating drama.

What's the difference? Story is drama. It's the focal character's moment-to-moment experience of each scene, which means the reader is living in their shoes, walking into the dimly lit bar with them, tasting the whiskey, seeing the outline of the gun in the bearded guy's pocket. As opposed to getting a history of the bar or the city where the bar is located or the saga of the focal character's complicated and deeply boring relationship with their mother.

Usually what this amounts to is the author deciding they must tell us all the things they think we need to know before the story can get started.

Whenever a client says to us, "I know the first four chapters are slow, but wait till you get to the fifth," we know *this* is the problem.

> *A common snag is when there is too much telling and summary in the opening chapters and writers try and cram in too much information without letting the story get going and unfold organically.*
> —Jill Marsal, Marsal Lyon Literary Agency

Yes, information and context are important; they bring depth to a story, and if you use them effectively, you can draw readers in. But if all you're doing is giving us information, we won't hang around. Information is dull. We can't visualize it. We can't enter it. It keeps us at arm's length. Whereas drama draws us in and makes us want to stay. What will happen when that guy with the beard pulls the gun out of his pocket? We simply must know.

What Is Narrative Context?

Narrative context is information. This is when you take a step away from the focal character's lived experience to tell us all those things you think we need to know. This context might look like summary or explanation. Sometimes it's a flashback. Sometimes it's a "convenient" scene that packages background information, as opposed to a scene that kicks off a significant sequence of events. But narrative context can be tricksy, as Gollum would say. It doesn't just show up in exposition. It can also creep into thought and sometimes even into dialogue.

If you think a reader won't notice this, think again.

Context via exposition

This is when the narrator explains or summarizes anything other than what's happening in the focal character's moment-to-moment experience of the scene. It's like the author is pausing the scene to bring readers up to speed. Imagine a movie stopping dead and the director stepping on screen to fill you in on all the things they think you need to know before the show can continue. Sound annoying? That's the effect you're creating every time you stop your story to deliver information.

Context via interiority

Interiority refers to anything that's going on inside the focal character's head—thoughts, observations, musings, and the like. What could be so wrong with that? Of course we want to know how the focal character is feeling, what they're thinking. Interiority draws us deeper into their experience of the present moment and helps us care about the character. But it can also become a sneaky way for the author to fill readers in with information and explanations. Not sneaky enough, unfortunately. Readers pick up on it immediately, mainly because it's boring.

Context via dialogue

This is the most glaring form of the infodump—when dialogue is stuffed with information for the reader's benefit, especially when it's something the other speaker already knows. It's a conversation that no two people in the history of the world would ever have. Dialogue has two jobs: to develop character and to advance the plot. Note that "informing the reader" is not part of that job description. When you force dialogue into that position, what you get is conversation that comes across as contrived and generally lacks tension. It might even sound like an interview.

Experience Versus Explanation

> *I want to feel like I'm a part of this world, so when you stop to take a page and a half to tell me about the inner workings of things, it doesn't feel like I'm living it.*
> —Beth Marshea, Ladderbird Literary Agency

We read, at least in part, to experience vicariously. That's the magic of good storytelling. It makes us feel like we're standing right next to the protagonist. We see how they react to what happens, we know what they think, smell what they smell. And perhaps most importantly: we know what they want. Not just a *meh, I'll take it if there's nothing else.* This is about yearning. It's about desperation. A protagonist's struggle to achieve a worthwhile and tangible goal is what keeps us turning pages.

What stops us? Blocks of summary and explanation. Every time you summarize or deliver information, you pull your reader out of the scene. When your explanation of some aspect of world history goes on for several sentences, paragraphs, even pages, our eyes are guaranteed to glaze over.

As Beth Marshea notes, too much information means she doesn't feel like she's living in the story. It breaks immersion. Your readers should be *experiencing* the story on every page. This is especially important in your opening chapter—i.e., the pages you're sending to whoever you hope will eventually buy or represent the manuscript.

When Context Shines

And yet... narrative context plays a critical role in fiction and narrative nonfiction. It adds depth to the characters, the setting, and the conflict. We need to know where and when we are. We need a place to stand in the fictional world, or else we can't participate in the scene.

So what are you supposed to do with crucial information that you simply must get across? The trick lies in subtlety. Be quick about it. Slip it in so that we don't notice. Resist the temptation to summarize and explain. Instead, focus all your energy on the focal character's senses, thoughts, and feelings, but allow at least some narrative context to be a question mark in the beginning—particularly the why. (Don't hold back on the where and when; that is information we need right away.)

In other words, make readers crave an answer to the why before you give it to them. Then, sprinkle context hints throughout the manuscript and trust your intuitive readers to pay attention and put the pieces together. This is where reader participation comes into play. We become detectives. It's our job to follow your hints and clues until we figure out the mystery— why a character behaves or feels a certain way, why they want what they want. When this information isn't spelled out, reading becomes a process of discovery.

Reader Context Versus POV Context

Some hints, clues, and clarifications about narrative context work better than others. If your snippet of context feels like something the focal character might say about what is happening in the scene (as an aside), then it's "POV context." But if it feels like explanation that's meant to fill us in, then it's "reader context." POV context can help build character and voice, whereas reader context is more like the author stepping in to interrupt the scene with information.

Ask yourself: is this snippet you're tempted to include directly relevant to what's happening RIGHT NOW in the scene? If not, hold on to it for later (or never).

Here's an example of what we mean:

Reader context: Jimmy walked into his office and plopped down in his chair. He was sixty-four years old and had been working as an architect for almost forty years now. His final contract was for a strip mall on the edge of town.

POV context: Jimmy walked into his office and plopped down at the drafting desk. He flipped open his agenda and reviewed his current project, a strip mall on the edge of a suburban wasteland. Six more months to see the project to completion and then he'd be able to retire.

In the first example, the context is offered up as flat information to fill us in. In the second, it's incorporated into Jimmy's moment-to-moment experience and sounds less like information and more like his voice.

Setup Versus Stasis

Many novels begin with stasis, a snapshot of the protagonist's regular life before it gets disrupted by the inciting incident. But stasis should not mean boring. It should have a source of tension, even if the main trajectory of the story has not yet been established. This is where we first meet your protagonist; you'll want them to make a good first impression—and by that we mean you want them to be memorable in some way. They should have personality, and they should want something.

Already? Yes, already. We all want something, all the time, whether we recognize it or not. Before the story gets started, your protagonist lived in the story world, doing something else with their life and wanting something long before the inciting incident comes around to kick their butt into high gear. That underlying motivation is what will crystallize into a narrative goal.

These are your opening pages. You need to transport readers into the story world right away and then give us a reason to stay, because we already show up to the page with plenty of reasons to leave. Life is distracting. If you start off with a summary of the protagonist's life or an explanation for why things are the way they are, you will guarantee that the reader (or agent, or publisher) will be reaching for their phone.

If this tempts you to skip stasis, you can. Many novels open with the inciting incident. Others, like *Moby-Dick* and *The Great Gatsby*, open even later. But to pull this off, you'll want to resist adding any early summary or explanation about whatever has set the protagonist in motion. Sure, give your readers hints about the inciting incident, but otherwise allow them to assemble that picture for themselves.

No Grocery Lists Allowed

As you evaluate your opening pages, consider each nugget of context you introduce. Is it essential, or are you trying to set up and explain? Strip your opening down to actions and descriptions that reveal character and setting and kick-start the story's conflicts. Each sentence should pull a literary agent into the story, making them forget they're reading a submission. You're aiming for a visceral experience, not a grocery list of information.

How to Write a Gripping First Chapter

As Ursula K. Le Guin wrote, "First sentences are doors to worlds." That's true whether you're writing the first line of a novel, chapter, or scene. The way you design your story's doorway determines whether we can trust where you will take us next, and whether we want to walk through.

A first chapter must grab an agent's attention right away. Overused openings—characters waking up, reviewing their appearance in mirrors—are likely to prompt a gigantic sigh from agents who have seen these things a thousand times. Similarly, chapters heavy on setup and explanation signal to agents that the manuscript is still undercooked. These elements don't just slow the pace; they are red flags that this writer is still learning to trust their reader.

Zoom Out Before You Zoom In

One common misstep we see in novel openings is the tendency to zoom in too tightly, too soon. If you begin in the middle of the action and focus on a minute detail or a single character's immediate experience, you might inadvertently cause a problem. Your readers will be busily filling in the blanks, and there's a good chance they'll be wrong.

What this causes is a jarring disruption of our immersion in the scene. We thought we knew where we were and who was present. When we discover that what seemed like an isolated setting is actually a crowded shopping mall, we're forced to recalculate, reset all our assumptions, start over.

Readers need to be grounded right away, which means you must establish two key elements up front: *space* and *occupancy*.

Space: Where is this scene unfolding?

Occupancy: Who or what is present?

To do that, you'll need a slightly wider lens so that we get an immediate sense of the environment and who's in it.

Starting with an abstract concept or emotion—without sensory details—can also work if you gradually illuminate the scene in the sentences that follow. This is a little like starting your readers off in the dark. If there is nothing for us to picture, then there's no way for you to lead us astray.

For example, if you opened a story with the statement "Jimmy always liked cats," you aren't yet inviting readers into a specific time and place, so there is nothing for us to mis-imagine. But when you do finally turn on the lights, the same principle applies: Give us space and occupancy as soon as possible. Don't let us jump to any incorrect assumptions.

Another example of opening with darkness is leading with a line of dialogue. But this can be tricky to pull off. The problem with dialogue is it demands a scene, even if we can't yet see it—there is a speaker and assumedly at least one listener. If you answer the first line of dialogue with a second, the reader has no sensory reference point, and they might get annoyed in a hurry. Still, anything can be done well.

Zooming In Too Quickly

Consider this hypothetical opening line:

She tightened her grip on the wheel, knuckles whitening as the strain grew unbearable.

What image blooms in your mind as you read this? Do you picture a woman alone in a car, driving in a high-speed chase? What if you learned in the next sentence that the vehicle is actually stopped, and her white-knuckle grip is because she just hit a pedestrian? Or if it turns out she's driving a school bus, and the cause of her strain is her rage at a horde of unruly children? Or the wheel in question is actually the helm on a sailboat in treacherous seas?

It's possible that the second sentence will provide the necessary clarification of space and occupancy, but it isn't a good idea to give your reader uncertainty for even one moment. This is especially true for the very first line of a novel or story. For the opening line of a new scene in an already established narrative, readers might be more forgiving, especially if they already have some context from the previous scene or chapter to guess at where the focal character might now be.

Ideally, your opening sentence should offer readers a helping hand so we can step into the focal character's experience without any bumps or snags. Holding back information at this stage is not a good way to create suspense. All it creates is confusion.

Famous Opening Lines and Why They Work

> *It was a queer, sultry summer, the summer they electrocuted the Rosenbergs, and I didn't know what I was doing in New York.*

In *The Bell Jar* by Sylvia Plath, we begin very zoomed out, with a note about the weather/season, a pervasive mood, and the fact that the narrator is in New York. We know generally where we are, and we meet the narrator right away.

> *We were somewhere around Barstow on the edge of the desert when the drugs began to take hold.*

Hunter S. Thompson's opening in *Fear and Loathing in Las Vegas* gives us another example of a wide-angle opening shot: somewhere on the edge of the desert, but a desert in the United States, as well as a general mood with the drugs kicking in. And while occupancy isn't totally clear, the "we" in this case suggests two people or a small group. It's open-ended enough to give readers a wisp of a scene, which the narrator can build on in the next line.

> *It was a bright cold day in April, and the clocks were striking thirteen.*

George Orwell's opening line in *Nineteen Eighty-Four* is so zoomed out as to be almost in the dark. We have the sensory input of light, cold weather, and a time of year, and the mood-establishing hint that something about this world is different than the one we know, with the unlucky number 13 adding a splash of tension.

> *As Gregor Samsa awoke one morning from uneasy dreams he found himself transformed in his bed into a gigantic insect.*

The opening line of Kafka's *Metamorphosis* starts a bit more zoomed in, and yet Gregor is waking up in his bedroom, so right away we've got space and occupancy. It's possible there is someone else in bed with him, but "his bed" suggests he's alone. Kafka gives us the mood of his uneasy dreams and the horror of the realization that he has transformed into an insect. In other words, it's very specific, but it's not so zoomed in that the next sensory detail will derail our mental image.

By contrast, if it turns out that his bed is a bottom bunk in a massive dormitory, readers will likely have imagined something different, so an immersion-breaking double take will ensue. This opening line wouldn't work for such a setting. It anticipates and relies on the reader's assumption that this is a quiet bedroom with nothing else going on apart from Gregor's nasty discovery.

> *Call me Ishmael.*

The opening line of Melville's *Moby-Dick* works wonders for a couple of reasons. It tells us what we ought to call the narrator (and not necessarily his name), which immediately hints at unreliability, and it also establishes a voice and reader address that will persist throughout the novel. No scenic detail here. We're starting out in darkness. Just note that you don't want to keep your reader in darkness for too long. That all-important immersion requires sensory detail.

Packing a Suitcase for Your Reader

During our MFA, author Annabel Lyon taught us to think about the opening pages of a novel like a suitcase you're packing for your reader. This is about setting the stage and establishing a few key expectations. What will they need on this journey? How can you best prepare them? Don't put things in the suitcase they'll never look at again. The opening is prime real estate. If you put something there, it better be important. As Annabel Lyon said, don't make your character drag around a hockey bag's worth of information. This suitcase should be more like a carry-on.

Keep in mind that the opening of a novel can be overwhelming to readers. They're stepping into a world that's familiar to you but unfamiliar to them. Your job is to ease the reader in and make the entry as smooth as possible. Don't inundate us with too many characters or too much information. Keep it simple.

Here are some other things to consider about what an opening should be doing in a novel:

1) That crucial first sentence should hook the reader

Your first sentence needs to be great. At the least, your opening line should establish voice, but bonus points if it can also "forecast" the novel in some way.

What do effective openings have in common? They create intrigue. They're hospitable. They make us want to read more.

We would bet that the famous first lines we mentioned above did not show up in first drafts. They were sweated over, reconsidered, and edited scores of times before being pronounced *just right*. Flaubert spoke of finding *le mot juste*—the exact right word. That's what you're looking for here. Something to pique a reader's attention and compel them to read the next sentence.

2) Start with your main character

Who you start the novel with is a clue to the reader about who will be important. The key people should appear as close to the opening as possible, and it therefore follows that anyone who isn't important doesn't deserve this prime position. If you find yourself having to refer to an insignificant character in the opening pages, don't name them.

3) Start in scene

The tendency for new authors is to want to tell readers all the things you think we need to know before the story can start. This is usually why prologues fail. Readers are smart. We need much less information than you think. Start in the story and trust that we'll catch on.

4) Establish the genre

Some surprises in a novel are good, but surprising your readers with a genre we didn't expect is not one of them. If you're writing fantasy, we should get a sense of that within the first few pages.

5) Establish the narrator's voice

We've already mentioned this in a previous chapter, but voice is the number one reason agents and publishers reject a manuscript, because it's the best barometer of whether you've brought a character to life or created a sock puppet. When fiction is described as having a great voice, it means the prose is distinct in a way that feels unique, with a narrator who gets right into the reader's head.

The key to tackling voice is knowing your narrator. If you have a clear idea of who your narrator is and how they speak, then you'll have a much easier time infusing the prose with their personality.

6) Create intrigue

Give your reader a reason to keep reading. Make the protagonist someone we want to get to know better. While it's important for us to know the who, what, where, and when as close to the start as possible, the why is something you can keep in your back pocket to kindle some mystery.

7) Hint at the theme

Theme answers the question *who cares?* It forms the bedrock of the novel and lets us know why we should keep turning pages.

8) Reveal the narrator's immediate intentions

Everyone wants something. Desire drives a story forward. Let the reader know what your protagonist wants in the opening scene—and, if possible, in the story as a whole.

9) Hint at the stakes

What does the protagonist stand to lose if they don't achieve what they're struggling and striving toward? The reader needs to know this fairly quickly, even if it's just suggested by the stasis.

10) Make your narrator relatable

For readers to want to follow your protagonist for hundreds of pages, we have to be able to see ourselves in this person somehow. Vulnerability goes a long way.

But... Don't Front-Load Your Opening Pages

Yes, we've just given you a long list of all the things that should show up in your opening in one form or another. So how are you supposed to get all this stuff in without front-loading your opening?

We didn't say this was easy. You get as much into your opening as you can by being subtle. By taking your time. By revising, and revising, and revising again—and then getting feedback and more feedback. When it comes to submitting work, most writers are in too much of a rush.

Avoid Clichéd Openers Like the Plague

Here are some openings agents see way too often:

- A character waking up
- Exposition
- The weather
- Dialogue that lacks context
- A long passage of description
- A fight scene (or bullying scene)
- A dream sequence
- Language that is too heavy and flowery

Consider the question *why today?* Why is this story starting here as opposed to somewhere else? What is it about this moment that makes it the best choice for your opening scene? In most cases, it should be as close as possible to the moment where everything changes for your protagonist.

If this all sounds picky and time-consuming, then you're taking it the right way. Your writing sample is the single most important thing you send an agent or publisher. It's the proof behind your sales pitch, and you don't get a second chance at it. If your queries are all being met with crickets, the chances of it being due to your writing sample are pretty damn close to one hundred percent.

Let's Get Practical: Investigating Immersion

Gather five of your favourite novels (or the best ones you have on hand). Reread the first page of each. Open a blank document or grab a pen and paper. Note up to five things from each first page that grab you. For example, how does the first sentence land? What is the initial image of character and/or setting? What pulls you in and makes you want to turn the page?

Once you have notes for five books, return to your manuscript. Imagine you are an agent who has just slogged through a difficult slush pile of queries that all missed the mark. The agent is tired and perhaps not as sharp at this point in the day. From this perspective, read your first page again. Note five things that will hopefully draw an agent in. Note five things that may elicit a cringe and a quick *nope*. Fix those things, then see if there are more.

Prologue Prejudice: The Good, the Bad, and the Rejected

With everything we write, we're essentially saying: we've got a great story to tell you, you'll be able to see yourself in it, and you won't be bored. It's a promise, and sometimes that promise begins with a prologue. But prologues, like any literary device, come with their own baggage. A rumour has been going around for some years now that agents and editors hate prologues—to the point where if they see one, it means immediate rejection. But is that true?

The answer is more nuanced than a simple yes or no. A prologue can either dazzle or disappoint; it can add depth to a narrative or disrupt it before it even gets off the ground.

Myths and Reality: Do Agents and Editors Really Hate Prologues?

The generalization that agents and editors hate prologues has emerged from a cocktail of publishing anecdotes, author forums, and rejection letters. However, like many "rules" in writing and publishing, the truth is a little more complicated.

What most agents and editors actually dislike are crappy prologues. Duh.

Take a look at almost any bestseller list and you'll likely find a novel on there that uses a prologue. Think of *A Game of Thrones* by George R.R. Martin or *The Da Vinci Code* by Dan Brown. In both cases, the prologue sets the novel's tone and creates intrigue exactly the way a well-written opening should.

According to a 2019 survey conducted by Reedsy, approximately thirty-four percent of traditionally published novels included prologues. Clearly not all publishers chant the "no prologues" mantra.

If your prologue is masterfully crafted and serves a distinct purpose, it's unlikely to be the sole reason for your manuscript's rejection. But a poorly conceived prologue can indeed send agents and editors running for cover. It's an early signal of trouble ahead.

The Perils of Prologues

What makes a prologue fall flat?

One of the biggest offenders is info-dumping. If you're using your prologue as an excuse to give us unnecessary backstory or explain world-building elements, know that you're starting at a huge disadvantage, which is namely that readers won't care. If we haven't had a chance to meet the characters and invest ourselves emotionally in their circumstances, we won't want to know where they're from and what kind of world they live in. Your number one job is to make us care. Information simply won't do that.

Keep in mind that your audience doesn't need to know everything up front. A bit of mystery, a few unanswered questions, and some gradual world-building are far more interesting than a lecture on the political situation of your world.

But say you're coming at this from a different angle: not to deliver information but to kick things off with a bang. Won't that work?

Usually: no. Another common misstep is when a writer throws in an action-packed prologue, hoping to compensate for a dull first chapter. Nice try. What you actually create is a jarring transition from action to information, along with a prologue that we (again) won't care about because we're not yet invested in the characters. Your first chapter should be able to stand on its own without having to depend on the prologue to create all the intrigue.

Another common pitfall is to be purposely vague in the prologue, to cloak it in mystery to entice the reader. In reality, when you drop us into a disorienting scene, we'll be confused rather than intrigued. It's a quick way to encourage your reader to put the book down.

When Prologues Shine

Despite these snags, prologues can work wonders when done right. A well-crafted prologue can set the tone, create intrigue, and provide readers with instant immersion.

But what distinguishes a successful prologue from a failed one? Essentially, the same features that distinguish a good first chapter: voice, causality, and strong sensory detail. Immerse us in a scene that matters and make us want to turn the page. Make us care.

The best prologues often have a specific job. This is especially true in genres like mystery, thriller, and fantasy. In a mystery novel, the prologue often provides a catalyst for the protagonist's inciting incident. This is usually the murder or crime to be investigated, or someone discovering the murder or crime scene. In thriller and fantasy, the prologue often gives us a glimpse of the antagonist doing their dastardly worst in a way that sets up the stakes.

In short, a good prologue sets the stage while also compelling readers to dive into chapter one.

Prologue Versus Chapter One: Weighing the Pros and Cons

Your opening pages are an opportunity to introduce your characters, your narrative voice, your setting, and your story. In many ways, chapter one has more heavy lifting to do than any prologue. So why divide your efforts between the two when you could write an extraordinary opening chapter?

The reality is that many agents and editors are wary of prologues, given how often they're mishandled. They want to dive straight into the story. When you begin with a strong first chapter, you have a better chance of delivering an immersive story right from the start.

If your queries are being met with silence, shake things up. See if you get a better response to a writing sample that begins with chapter one rather than a prologue.

The Importance of Feedback: On Alpha and Beta Readers, Critique Partners, and Editors

Back when we met at an MFA novel-writing workshop, we had a teacher who insisted that "writing is rewriting." It's not a happy thought, but in our experience it's definitely true. Writing the first draft of a novel is the fun part, and it's usually the quickest part as well. Then you have to roll up your sleeves and turn your mess of a manuscript into something that's good enough to meet the world.

The trouble is, when you're preparing to send out a manuscript to agents or publishers, "good enough" is *not* good enough. You have to set the bar much higher than that. But it's not always easy to tell when your manuscript is ready to go or when you're still dealing with those two Cs you don't want: chaos and confusion. As we like to say, a great novel is honed, not hatched. And to hone your novel, you need feedback.

Luckily, that's pretty easy to find these days. But feedback can come in many forms. So what's the difference between alpha readers, beta readers, critique partners, and developmental editors? Let's get into it.

Alpha Readers: Nurturing a New Narrative

An alpha reader is the first person to read your brand-new manuscript. You've gone through the initial stages of self-editing, and you're finally ready for those early eager eyeballs.

The idea here is that your manuscript is still in a raw state. The first people you turn to for feedback will likely know you well. Maybe it's your spouse or your best friend. Ideally, it will be someone who can give you a big-picture assessment, but more importantly, they will be gentle and encouraging.

Keep in mind that readers who know you and your voice will have an easier time sinking into your writing and will also have a vested interest in your success. That's why alpha feedback can only take you so far. Once you've addressed this initial stage of helpful suggestions, it's time to turn to people who will give you a more objective perspective.

Beta Readers: The Bookish Bystanders

Do beta readers always follow alpha readers? Not necessarily. Some writers go straight to a developmental editor at this stage. But an editor's feedback will be more substantive than what you will tend to receive from alpha or beta readers. Whether an editor takes on your manuscript immediately after your alpha readers or later on, beta readers are still considered the second round of *reader* feedback.

Beta readers should be people you don't know, or at least not well. Perhaps they're already familiar with your work, but they should be willing to give you unflinchingly honest feedback. That's not to say they shouldn't also be encouraging. Good feedback, after all, emphasizes what's working along with what isn't. The point is, at this stage you want feedback that's more impartial—from people who don't have a stake in your success.

Readers Versus Editors

At a general level, an editor has a strong grasp of craft fundamentals like trajectory, characterization, structure, pacing, and stakes, whereas a reader's focus is more likely to be their personal preferences, engagement, and expectations. The alpha/beta reader says, "Here is my experience of the text," while a good editor will say, "Here is my assessment of a potential reader's experience of the text."

A professional editor should be able to tell you not only that something is (or isn't) working, but they should also be able to explain why. It's easy to have a knee-jerk reaction when someone says they don't like something you've written. Much harder when a person can explain on a craft level why your approach is likely to break reader immersion or won't create the necessary emotional draw to make a reader care about your story.

What About Critique Partners?

Just to make things more confusing, critique partners are usually other writers with whom you exchange feedback. They might be members of your writing group or random writer friends you've connected with on social media.

Critique partners are really no different from beta readers. Or not necessarily—if you're married to a novelist or your critique partner is a dev editor. Don't get too caught up in these terms. The takeaway is simple: get as much feedback as possible from a wide variety of sources. We write to be read, so the reader's experience of our work is the only barometer we have.

Recruitment and Selection

If you don't have any family or friends eager to read a fledgling manuscript (it's a big ask, after all), your first readers are more likely to be from the beta camp.

When choosing beta readers, look for people who are familiar with your genre and are willing to be honest, yet supportive. They don't necessarily need to be experts in the craft, but they should understand what makes a story engaging and be able to explain how they feel about your manuscript.

Obviously, if you're hiring beta readers, you should be more careful about who you ask. A volunteer might not feel obliged to finish the job, so you'll want to cast a wide net. Also, keep in mind how much time and effort it takes to read a manuscript and deliver feedback. If you send your beta volunteers a tip or a small gift, they'll be more likely to work with you again.

Yes, there is such a thing as free beta readers. There are subreddits and Goodreads groups you can join. And there's always social media. Ask around. Pitch your story. Finding free beta readers usually requires some effort, some engagement, and quite often a trade—*I'll read your book if you read mine*. So be prepared to return the favour.

Are Beta Readers Safe?

The short answer is generally, yes, beta readers are quite safe, and most authors use them without any issues.

Sure, it's possible for a beta reader to steal your manuscript or your ideas, but it would be difficult. First of all, proving copyright is quite simple in the digital era. Second, anyone can "borrow" your ideas, but only a talented writer will be able to bring them to life. If they put in that amount of effort, the final product isn't likely to resemble your story anyway.

This is another benefit of hiring professional beta readers—their reputation is on the line, so you can expect both discretion and integrity. That being said, buyer beware. With the advent of GenAI, some beta readers are "delegating" their efforts to Chatbot. Ask for a guarantee before you commit.

Get Feedback in Some Form

Whatever path you take, before you start querying, it's imperative that you get feedback in some form. You simply won't have the objectivity necessary to evaluate your own manuscript, and as a result, it won't be ready to meet the world.

- "It is very clear when we receive a manuscript that is at an early stage of drafting," said Kerry D'Agostino (Curtis Brown, Ltd.).
- "Most projects I receive are at too early a stage for me to offer representation," said Jennifer March Soloway (Andrea Brown Literary Agency).
- "I see many projects that have potential but they're not close enough to being marketable for me to take on," said BJ Robbins (BJ Robbins Literary Agency).

Do you sense a pattern here? You only get one chance with an agent, so don't blow it by submitting your manuscript before it's truly ready. Agents aren't interested in taking on work that still needs a big overhaul. They need to know that you have what it takes to put in the long hours and keep pushing until your manuscript is as good as it can possibly be. For this reason, it's critical that most of that work is done before your query hits their inbox.

This doesn't mean you have to follow every feedback recommendation you receive without question—far from it. But it's crucial to entertain all feedback and consider how you might approach your manuscript from a different angle.

If there is a secret to getting published, it's feedback, feedback, and more feedback. But how much is enough? That depends on who's giving it to you and how much experience they have. If the readers you're using don't have much expertise or are only giving you feel-good feedback, you won't improve.

This is not about feeling good. It's about learning how to write. Do the hard thing. Get objective feedback from a variety of sources. Swallow your pride—and revise.

Let's Get Practical: How Do Your First Pages Land?

The point of this activity is to get out of your head and try to imagine your manuscript's first pages from an external perspective. This is an important component of self-critique.

Read aloud: This is something you should do with your entire manuscript. It's a great way to catch sneaky typos, errors in logic, repetitions, and clunky dialogue.

Have your computer read the manuscript aloud: There are many programs and even websites that can help you with this (Microsoft Word can do it). Even though computer voices and AI reading can be robotic and awkward, they're still a great way to hear your work from a slightly different perspective. This is also helpful for catching errors and assessing both rhythm and pacing.

Read as your enemy: Imagine you are someone who's been unfairly critical of you in the past. Try to get inside their head, then read your first pages from that perspective. What would they hate? What would it take to impress them?

Read over a shoulder: Have a friend or family member who has not previously seen your manuscript sit down and quietly read your opening pages. Stand behind them and read along. This is another great way to force yourself to consider your work from an external perspective.

Querying Strategically

You've done it. You've written a query letter that makes your novel sound fresh, a must read, and that makes you sound like you know your market. Your synopsis shows that you understand both structure and arc. You've sought feedback and have rewritten the manuscript so many times you feel like you could recite it from memory. Good. You're ready to begin the hunt for representation.

So—where do you start?

1) Identify the top ten agents you'd like to work with

Make sure your manuscript fits their criteria, particularly that it's a genre they represent.

2) Set these agents aside for later

That's right. Do NOT query them. Few writers land representation in the first five or ten queries they send out, and you only get one chance with each agent, so don't blow your first round of submissions on the best of the best.

Make a new list of five to ten suitable agents and start with these instead.

3) Send out five queries... and wait

Keep in mind that an agent's priority is their clients. They generally don't read queries as they roll in. More likely, their submission box fills, and they only get to it when they have a spare minute in between reading new drafts or revisions from their current client list. Which is why you don't want to do anything to piss them off right from the start—like phoning them or spamming them with emails asking why you haven't heard back from them yet.

Wait at least two weeks. If you haven't heard anything back, send out five new queries.

4) Wait... and revise

Once you have ten queries out in the world, and you've given the agents a few more weeks to poke at their slush piles, it's time to go back to the revision desk. Tweak your query letter. Have another look at your opening pages. Now that time has given you some distance, is there anything you might tighten or improve? Is there another opening scene that might be more effective at grabbing their attention?

5) Resubmit

Keep searching out more agents who might be a good fit and follow the same submission pattern—five at a time.

The reasoning behind this trickle approach is simple: if there's something in your submission that's putting people to sleep, you don't want to burn through fifty or a hundred possibilities before you realize it. Treat each set of five submissions as a test. If none of these agents asks to read your full manuscript, it means you still have work to do.

6) And then, finally, you get a full request

Awesome! An agent has asked to read your full manuscript. Cross your fingers, send it off, and open a bottle of wine or a box of chocolates. This isn't success—not necessarily—but it's a big step forward.

THIS is the moment you've been waiting for. As soon as you send off the manuscript, jump on those top agents you've been keeping in your back pocket. You finally know your submission package has the potential to catch an agent's eye. Now the real hunt begins.

7) And wait...

Remember, this is a long road. Some agents will take a year or more to read your query letter. Some will take equally as long to read your complete manuscript. As we mentioned before, an agent's priority is their current client list. This may seem frustrating, but once you've finally landed representation, you'll appreciate your agent's attention and responsiveness.

8) Keep writing

Yes, we've said this before, and we will keep saying it. Writing is a craft. You get better at it by doing it. You might think you're already good at it, but we promise you that if you keep writing, ten years from now you'll look back at the work you're doing today and cringe.

You will never know all there is to know about writing. There will never come a time when you can't find room for improvement. Keep attending conferences and workshops, keep getting feedback, keep reading, and keep pushing yourself to get better.

Should You Find a Literary Agent or Self-Publish? (Pssst—There's a Third Option)

Should you get a literary agent? How long should you query a project before you quit? Is it really better to self-publish these days? What's your best path forward to publication and book sales?

These are all good questions, and of course the answer is, "It's complicated," but it's worth considering the pros and cons of each publishing path. It's likewise important to recognize that querying and self-publishing are not the only options.

In fact, there are three main publication paths you might take as a writer:

1) finding a literary agent to represent your manuscript to the major publishers,
2) finding a smaller publisher directly, without the help of an agent, and
3) self-publishing.

What Is Indie Publishing?

Indie or independent publishing used to mean a small publisher that wasn't owned or controlled by a corporate entity. Then people started using it to describe publishing services for self-published authors. Imagine a company that helps you get your manuscript from a Word document into an e-reader format and listed on Amazon. But more and more, indie is being used interchangeably with self-publishing. Since the definition isn't clear, we won't use it here.

The Pros and Cons of Self-Publishing

Self-publishing gives you the most freedom and the biggest cut of your book sales. You have complete artistic control. You will never have an editorial committee demand that you change your title or kill off a character. You get to decide what the cover will look like. And every sale represents a success of your story as well as your marketing prowess. But this also means you don't get that kind of input from professionals who might know more about these things than you do.

It's much easier to self-publish a book than it is to land a publishing deal, at least initially. However, when you self-publish, you need to master a lot more than writing an immersive and engaging story. You need to be adept at marketing and networking. You also need a reliable team of trusted readers and/or professional editors to ensure your manuscript is the best it can be.

Worst-case scenario? If you rush to self-publish, you may end up with a book that doesn't sell and that, with time, becomes a stain on your writerly reputation. We've worked with many clients who have come to regret a hastily self-published novel, so they pull it off Amazon and start the editing process from scratch.

What Do Literary Agents Do?

A literary agent can be many things, but first and foremost they represent you in the publishing world. They negotiate contracts (book deals) with publishers who do not accept submissions directly from authors. In other words, literary agents are gatekeepers for the heavyweight book industry.

An agent can be a powerful addition to your team. Many of them are excellent editors who will help you sharpen your manuscript before sending it out on submission. (Yes, it's true, the editing never ends.) They will champion your efforts and offer their industry expertise along the way. Agents may also be marketing experts, but that's not necessarily the case. Marketing is the publisher's job, though the author is also expected to participate in this role—presenting at conferences and webinars, doing book signings, engaging with fans via social media, and more.

In exchange for their assistance, expertise, and connections, agents receive a percentage of their authors' earnings—usually ten to twenty percent.

Pros and Cons of Agented Publishing

The term *traditional publishing* often refers to the scenario involving literary agents and the Big Five publishers, but small publishers are also part of that tradition. So instead of *traditional*, let's call this *agented publishing*.

"How do I get an agent?" It's usually the first question asked of any author who has one. And sure, it's great to have one, but they are hard to get. The truth is, there's a horde of writers querying out there, and an agent's roster tends to grow slowly.

Agents often complain that the Big Five publishers have a stranglehold on the industry. Every year, there are fewer imprints and thus fewer acquisitions editors that agents can approach with submissions. On top of that, the Big Five's current marketing approach is to spend big on advertising when a new book comes out—but if early sales aren't immediately strong, they slash the marketing budget, and you're left shouldering the burden yourself: arranging events, courting independent bookstores, and trying to generate support without institutional backing.

What this means in practical terms is that you can do everything right— nail your query submission, land an agent, nab a publishing contract—and then get dropped. Worse, your poor sales could directly impact the size of your next advance or whether the publisher will even consider the sequel you were working on.

Another scenario: You land your dream agent and figure it's a straight shot to publication. It isn't. They might like your manuscript, but that doesn't mean they'll be able to convince any publishers to take a chance on you. Having an agent is only a step on the way to publication; it by no means guarantees it will happen.

Can You Get an Agent After Self-Publishing?

While it's generally not possible to find a literary agent to represent a novel that's already been self-published, there's nothing stopping you from finding representation for your next manuscript. In fact, having a self-published novel or memoir with decent sales and reviews can go a long way towards convincing an agent and publisher that you have a ready-made platform.

Pros and Cons of a Small Press

A small publisher is... small. It's often run by a handful of people, and they might only come out with ten or twenty titles per year. Because they don't have to kneel to any corporate overlord or follow their fickle marketing formulas, small publishers are generally more flexible, more personable, and more likely to take a chance on something that would not get past the gatekeepers of the Big Five.

Bonus: you don't need an agent to submit your manuscript to a small publisher.

Because they're small, however, they don't have a lot of money. Author advances tend to be lower (sometimes zero), and any book tour you do will likely be at your expense. However, small presses are more likely to keep promoting a book even if the initial sales are lower than expected. Also, the royalty percentage from small publishers tends to be more generous, and authors who don't mind taking an active role in marketing can sometimes negotiate for a better rate on the sales they drive themselves.

But not all small publishers are created equal. They can be excellent, but they can also be fly-by-night operations with very little budget. What suffers: your exposure to reviewers and awards juries, the quality of your cover, the level of their editorial input. Before you agree to hand your manuscript over to them, you need to do your homework. What other titles have they published? Have any been successful? Are their books well edited? Do they have quality cover art? Do they submit their books for awards? Do their books get reviewed?

If you aren't sure, ask to speak to one of their clients so you can get a sense of their experience. Or look up a few of their authors and contact them directly. You can also find feedback about publishers (and agents) on forums like the Absolute Write Water Cooler.

The Small Press Is on the Rise

The corporate publishing industry has been tightening its belt for years. Almost every agent we've interviewed points to this troubling trend. The result: fewer gatekeepers, less diversity, and rampant turnover.

Meanwhile, the small press is on the rise, both in terms of proliferation and prestige. As the big publishers focus purely on profit, we're seeing more small press titles nominated for esteemed honours like the Man Booker Prize. If the top continues to stifle itself, we can dare to hope that the rest of the industry will rise to the occasion.

Dealing with Rejection

Rejection is going to happen—a lot—so it's best to be prepared for it rather than being sidelined. Many authors we work with expect an easy turnaround of a few drafts and then... abracadabra, overnight success. If by overnight you mean ten years, then sure, maybe. Otherwise, you're looking at a long, steep road of learning and a lot of *nopes* along the way. You might think that isn't what you signed up for—but surprise, it is.

There's a lot to be said for managing your expectations. If you hire a professional editor to give you feedback, that will be your first experience with hearing some hard truths. You won't like it. You will probably think the editor is stupid or *just doesn't get it*. You'll be tempted to ignore their advice to rethink, to start over. You'll think they're exaggerating when they say it takes many drafts to get a novel right, and even then, you might not sell it.

Probably the biggest indicator of success in this business is an author's willingness to listen to feedback and then do the hard work of revision. Here's the reality: if you're not prepared to throw a draft in the garbage, you probably won't find an agent or a publisher for your work.

No, But... and No, Because...

But it's not all rejection.

Sometimes what you'll hear from an agent or publisher is a *no, but. No, this isn't quite for us, but we like your writing; please send more.* This is not something agents and publishers say to everyone, so if they say it to you, take them up on their offer.

What's most helpful is to hear a *no, because. No, this isn't working, and here's why.*

Unfortunately, most agents are so busy that they don't have time to tell you why they said no. This is a shame. You'll never know if it's because they read five dog stories in a row and yours was just bad timing, or if your work really isn't ready.

Be Willing to Listen

One of our editing clients recently asked us how we approach the process of revision.

When we get a *no, because* response, we usually spend the first few days railing about how that agent doesn't know anything, and we refuse to listen to their recommendations. Then we calm down and realize that agents and editors are not stupid. In fact, they know a lot, and if they didn't understand our work, the fault *might* lie elsewhere... namely with us.

We read the feedback many times. We might even print it out. We sit with it. We walk away from it and then come back, take some notes. We spend a lot of time thinking. We wait until there's a willingness inside us to consider new directions, new ideas. A willingness to throw out certain scenes and completely revise others. A willingness, in short, to listen.

Before we start the actual rewriting, we work out a synopsis in which we tell the whole (new) story from start to finish, making sure it hangs together and that we've addressed all the feedback we've received. If we have questions, we contact the editor or agent and ask them.

We also don't work in a vacuum. We have several other writers whom we rely on to tell us if we've put our pants on backwards in a manuscript, and we do the same for them. We can't stress enough how important it is to have a small team of people who tell you the truth and save you from embarrassment. We wouldn't dream of sending something out without their eyes on it first.

Listen to your editors and critique partners. Listen to that gem of an agent who took the time to give you some feedback. Be willing to consider revision in its truest form, as a way of reenvisioning your story with new eyes. It's hard, yes. But this is where the real writing begins.

And keep sending out your work. Better your story sits on an agent's desk than on yours.

100 Rejections a Year

This idea comes from a post on Literary Hub written by Kim Liao several years ago. Rather than dreading rejection, flip the process on its head and seek it out. Aim to get 100 rejections in a year. Spread your net wide. Send out stories, poems, novels. Apply for grants, residencies, fellowships. Look for an agent. Anything that expands your role in the literary world is fair game.

Not only does this mean you'll be getting your work out there and increasing the odds that someone will eventually say yes, it's also a complete change of attitude. It takes the dread out of the submission process and turns it into a challenge.

Dare we say it might even make it fun?

The Full Request

Success! An agent or publisher has responded with a request for your full manuscript. Suddenly, you're panicking.

Maybe the manuscript isn't quite ready—or not as ready as you thought. But now that someone has requested a full, you feel you have to rush to send it to them because of course they're waiting on pins and needles for your project.

But are they?

What do you think will happen if you take your time and send them the best manuscript you can? We've heard from several agents who have said they'd much rather wait for a great manuscript than get an average one right away.

If someone asks for your full manuscript, DON'T RUSH. Give the agent an ETA, then go over the manuscript one more time. You need to make it as good as it can be, and now that you know the next eyes on your pages will be an agent's, you might spot a few issues that evaded your previous revision efforts. You only get one shot with each agent or publisher. Don't blow it.

The Long Wait

You send out the manuscript—and then what?

The proverb "a watched pot never boils" is useful here. If all you're doing is sitting around waiting for that agent or publisher to respond, it will feel long, and it's not a productive way to spend your time. Instead, get busy. If that agent or publisher hasn't insisted on an exclusive read, go back to the other people who might still be sitting on your work and let them know the full manuscript is now being considered somewhere. Light a small fire under their feet. Create some momentum.

In fact, if you've held back on sending the manuscript to your top choices, now's the time to get it out there.

Start Something New

The best way to pass this anxious waiting period is by starting a new project. Hone your craft. This way, if the agent or publisher passes on this manuscript but says they'd love to read more of your work, you'll soon have something new to send them.

What Happens After Yes

It's a writer's dream. You open that email or get that phone call from a publisher or agent with the big news: they love your novel. It's actually going to happen, after years of heartache, years of relatives asking you when your book is coming out, and probably also carpal tunnel syndrome from so much typing.

That day, the day you get the news, is huge. You'll probably cry. You'll think your life is going to change. People will recognize you on the street. Writing your next book will be so much easier. You'll lose those ten pounds.

Ummm. No. Or, rather, not entirely.

One thing that does change is the feeling of validation. Usually, by the time you get that *yes*, you've got a lot of rejection under your belt. *No* gets heavy after a while. It doesn't feel good to carry it around. *No* can sink you. In that way, the *yes* makes a huge difference.

But in that way only. That one *yes* doesn't mean you now have a publisher for life who will accept every golden word you write. You're only as good as the book you're writing right now. Every time you write something new, you're essentially starting over. What you've done before doesn't matter, although what you've learned from it definitely does.

It Might Get Easier, but It Never Gets Easy

As your knowledge of the craft expands, you get better at putting a novel together. But we would never call it easy. We're now able to see the flaws in our work much faster and head them off at the synopsis stage, rather than throwing out hundreds of pages of work. But we're not going to lie— both of us have thrown out hundreds of pages before, and we will likely do so again.

One pitfall to beware of is the tendency to write the same book over and over. Start book two and you'll see what we mean. The plot points will be oddly similar to your first book. Even the subject matter might be similar. You'll get halfway through and think, *Damn, this seems a little too familiar.*

Regardless of how well your first book does, there will suddenly be pressure on you for the second book that you've never experienced before. If the first book did well, you'll feel pressured to measure up to that success. If it did poorly, you'll feel anxious about improving so the publisher will take the next one.

There are things that happen after you get the phone call that other writers don't often mention. The stress of the editorial process is one of them. After the glacial pace of querying, all of a sudden things move quickly, and you'd better be prepared to drop everything and meet your deadlines. By the time you proofread the galleys, you will be so sick of your book, you'll never want to see it again. You certainly won't want to read it again.

Exciting... and Terrifying

One night you'll wake up in a sweat with the realization that this novel, which has existed more or less as a secret in your life, will now be out in the world for anyone to read. You might think this is exciting, and it is. But it's also terrifying. There will be reviews. Not all of them will be good. Or worse, there won't be reviews. No one will care.

Chances are quite good that no one will recognize you on the street after your first novel is published. Movie producers won't line up outside your door, begging for the screen rights. The blank page will still be blank.

But... you've done it. Your name is out there now, and that's powerful. You might wander into a random bookstore and see your book on the shelf. And there's the value of experience. You'll take what you've learned and bring it to the next project. That project will kick your butt all over again, but in a different way, and you'll have something new to bring to the table for the project after that.

Is It Worth All the Heartache?

If you hesitated for even a second over that question, then the answer is probably no. There are easier ways to earn a living. But if you're compelled to keep writing even if a publication deal never materializes, then the heartache is just another part of the process.

After all, the process is as important as the outcome. In fact, we'd even say it's more important. If you don't love the process, you're in for a rough ride.

But if you do, then the outcome is a bonus. You get to sit at your desk, or in a café, or in a broom closet during your lunch hours, and work on this glorious idea you've had bouncing around in your head for months or even years. You get to live with characters you've created and experience a world of your making in intricate detail. You get to create something that would not exist in the world but for you.

There's nothing quite like it.

In Conclusion: Keep Writing

On average, I receive about three to five queries a day, so... out of the approximately fifteen hundred [I read per year], I probably request one to two percent. And of those... maybe [I represent] a handful.
—Karly Caserza (Fuse Literary)

This is a long road. Agents are slow to respond, and very few writers find representation for the first manuscript they write. Even if you end up with a great agent, there's no guarantee they'll sell your manuscript. So keep learning. Keep up the daily writing habit. If you expect instant success, you're likely to be crushed by failure. Instead, just as you treat each round of query submissions as a test, treat each manuscript you write as an experiment.

People will tell you that this is a highly subjective business and that somewhere, somehow, there's an agent who will fall in love with your manuscript. That is often untrue. Yes, persistence is important—there may well be one agent out there who will light up at your pitch. However, persistence in querying is not the same as persistence in writing, rewriting, and the endless quest for self-critique and self-improvement.

The other thing it's important to do is read. Read in your genre and outside of it. Read the classics—they are classics for a reason. Read like a writer—first to enjoy the work, second to study it and evaluate how the author achieved their results. Find books that are doing something similar to what you hope to do and use them as guides. Learn from them.

Take classes, talk to other writers, get feedback—and give it.

There are many guides out there with advice on how to write great query letters and how to effectively target the right agents, but the single most important step is to refine your narrative and polish your prose until your manuscript stands out among that top two percent of submissions that make an agent intrigued, then interested, then eager and excited to work with you.

No one is going to take a chance on your writing unless it's good enough—you must prove that you deserve it. If you love this process, don't lose hope. Dedicated hard work and a commitment to learning will pay off.

Appendix 1:
Resource Reviews

There are many online resources available to writers that can help make the querying process just a little simpler. Here are a few of our favourites.

Query Tracker

QueryTracker.net is an incredible database and querying tool. They keep very up-to-date records of all known literary agents—whether they are currently accepting submissions and which genres they represent. On top of that, once you're logged in, you can track whom you have queried, which agents have responded, and how much time has passed since your last interaction.

QueryTracker.net offers both free and paid memberships. The free option is very generous and meets most people's needs without an upgrade to premium. A premium membership gets you added search functions, the ability to track multiple projects, and several other features.

Of all the querying tools out there, QueryTracker.net is at the top of the heap.

Manuscript Wish List – #MSWL

Manuscript Wish List is an amazing tool that helps authors target and personalize their queries. It's both a website (manuscriptwishlist.com) and a hashtag (#MSWL). The concept is simple: agents share topics and story ideas they'd like to see in their query inbox.

The website hosts agent profiles and runs a newsletter for authors. You can also search Bluesky for the #MSWL hashtag. (Most agents have left X behind, but you can still find some of them on there.) You can do combined searches for an agent's handle and the hashtag or just go to the site and search for the agent. Also, the agent bios on here are sometimes more extensive than on agency websites, and they might include other tidbits like favourite books, fun facts, and submission guidelines.

Social Media Writing Communities

If you're an author trying to bring attention to your project or build an audience in the lead-up to your project, social media can be a helpful tool.

Once upon a time, the writing community on Twitter was the go-to place for writers to connect, network, find beta readers and book reviewers, and market their books. However, along came a certain billionaire who purchased the platform, gave it a new name, and changed most of the rules. Since then, the Twitter writing community has flagged. There are many diehards holding on, hoping for everything to return to how it was before, but many have fled to other platforms, namely Bluesky, Threads, and Instagram (Bookstagram). BookTok (on TikTok) is also worth checking out.

In the world of social media, nothing is static. Algorithms change. Platforms rise and fall in popularity. The marketing efficacy of these tools can also change. It used to be that a Facebook author page was gold for driving book sales. Now, most indie authors we work with rely on their blog and/or newsletter for most of their sales. Some find success running ad campaigns on Amazon. Social media? Not so much.

The labyrinth of book marketing is beyond the scope of this book. The point is—yes, some people figure it out and drive massive sales over social media, but most struggle to be heard. That said, social media is still good for finding and building community. And even if having strong social media muscles doesn't make you a shoo-in for bestseller lists, it can show agents and publishers that you're capable of generating interest and engaging with an audience. It can also lead to some great connections. Writing is a lonely art, and networking can open many doors.

Publishers Marketplace

Publishers Marketplace is a paid resource used by many industry professionals. Members get access to a wealth of information that is often not available elsewhere and certainly not all in one place. For example, they have extensive listings of who represents whom, deal reports with manuscript sales data, contact information for thousands of agents, editors, and more.

We wouldn't describe this as a must-have for querying authors, but many people do find it useful. Membership is month to month, so there's no long-term commitment.

Appendix 2:
Let's Get Personal

David's Story: Accept That You're on a Long Road

Fifteen years and counting. That's how long David has been chasing a traditional deal. His first full-length manuscript, *The Rippled Pond*, went out to agents in 2008. One agent liked the premise and voice but told him he'd built 20,000 words of setup and needed a ground-up rewrite. He shelved it and wrote other manuscripts that gathered even less attention. Then he entered the UBC MFA program, resurrected *The Rippled Pond*, and rewrote it from scratch. Not one sentence survived. Even then, more than a hundred queries led nowhere.

He kept writing.

Travel adventures sparked a new idea. He wrote *Sky to Sea*, a coming-of-age story about a girl escaping her father, the commander of a lunar prison. That one finally caught an agent's eye. Valerie Noble offered representation, they revised together, and the manuscript went out on submission. Every publisher passed. A few sent it to second readers, then backed away with the same line: *we just can't quite imagine a market for this.*

He kept writing.

Next, he built a four-book series set in an alternate-Earth equivalent of North Korea. Valerie said he had "levelled up," but the acquisitions editors still passed. His prose leaned too literary for the YA market. Or the characters skewed too old. Or something else no one could articulate.

He moved to adult fiction and wrote *Sleeping Cutie and the Destruction of Southgate Mall*, a speculative novel narrated by a cat named Doom. The Canada Council for the Arts awarded him a New Artist grant. Small presses showed interest, even asked for exclusivity, then ghosted. Again came the refrain: *we just can't quite imagine a market for this.*

He kept revising, built an editing and beta team, studied book marketing, and shifted to indie publishing. *Sky to Sea* took on a new title, *When the Sky Breaks*, and became his debut. After that, he shifted genres and published a fantasy satire called *We've Come for Your Eggs*. Meanwhile, *Sleeping Cutie* is on the desk of yet another acquisitions editor, and David is ready to start querying an exciting project in the new year.

A long road only leads somewhere if you stay on it.

Michelle's Story: Rewrite, Rewrite, Rewrite

Michelle wrote two "practice" novels before deciding to leap into the world of YA fantasy fiction, a world she knew precisely nothing about. She wrote the first draft of her manuscript in a dizzying six weeks. It then took ten years before she found a publisher.

During those ten years she did more ground-up rewrites than she can count.

She found an agent for her work, who asked her to rewrite the novel several more times and, in the end, gave up on the project because she couldn't find a publisher. When Michelle asked for the list of publishers who had seen it, it was surprisingly short and didn't include any small presses. So Michelle decided to try selling it herself.

After numerous *Dear Writer* rejections, one small press agreed to take it on—and then changed their mind (after she'd informed family and friends that her novel was finally being published). But one thing the editor did do was offer specific and extremely helpful feedback. Which meant... back to the drawing board and another ground-up rewrite.

By this time, the novel was so different from the original that Michelle felt it was fair game to approach the same publishers who'd said no years before. That turned out to be a good decision, because one of them finally said yes.

Her advance: zero.

Her editor: brilliant.

The experience: absolutely worth it.

That book eventually led to another novel with a larger press, which led to another agent. But it took an ungodly amount of perseverance and a willingness to keep reseeing the manuscript with different eyes, keep learning, keep trying, keep writing.

This doesn't mean her agent automatically accepted everything she wrote. Since then, she's been sent back to the drawing board on three projects and has no doubt there are more novels in her future that will need to be burned to the ground before they succeed.

But here's the key: every time you start over, you're still taking a step forward, and every revision brings you closer to the manuscript's best version of itself. It might sound painful or even depressing, but two of her published novels resulted from that very process and likely would never have seen the light of day had she not made drastic changes.

It's all part of the process.

About the Authors

Michelle Barker is an award-winning author and a senior editor with the Darling Axe. Her most recent novel *My Long List of Impossible Things* (2020, Annick Press) is a Junior Library Guild gold standard selection. *The House of One Thousand Eyes* (2018, Annick Press) won numerous awards, including the Amy Mathers Teen Book Award, and was named a Kirkus Best Book of the Year. She is also the author of *A Year of Borrowed Men*, finalist for the TD Canadian Children's Literature Award. Her poetry, short fiction and non-fiction have been published in literary reviews around the world. Michelle lives in Vancouver, Canada, on the unceded territories of the Musqueam, Squamish, and Tsleil-Waututh nations. Find her at MichelleBarker.ca.

David Griffin Brown is an award-winning short fiction writer with over twenty years' experience as an editor. He founded DarlingAxe.com in 2018, which has grown into a collective of industry experts, dev editors, line editors, proofreaders, and beta readers, with specialists across all genres. His spec fiction novels include *When the Sky Breaks* and *We've Come for Your Eggs*. He holds a BA in anthropology and an MFA in creative writing. David lives in Victoria, Canada, on the traditional territory of the Esquimalt and Songhees Nations. Find him at SeptimusBrown.com and on social media under the handles @SeptimusBrown and @DarlingAxe.

David and Michelle are co-authors of *Immersion and Emotion: The Two Pillars of Storytelling* and *Story Skeleton: The Classics*.